# MEDITERRANEAN DIET COOKBOOK FOR BEGINNERS

600-Days Quick, and Easy Blue-Zones Recipes to Change your Eating Lifestyle and Live Better! **28-Day Meal Plan** to get started!

## NAOMI LANE

# Table *of* Content

# Mediterranean Diet Pyramid

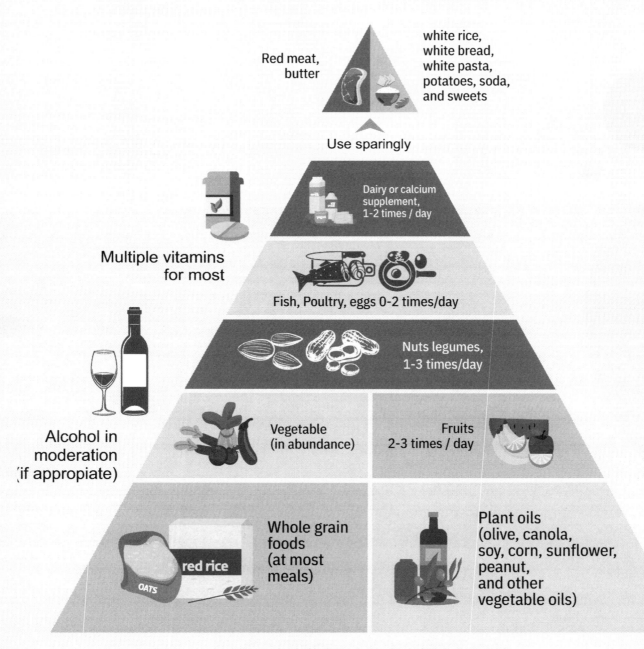

Red meat, butter — white rice, white bread, white pasta, potatoes, soda, and sweets

Use sparingly

Dairy or calcium supplement, 1-2 times / day

Multiple vitamins for most

Fish, Poultry, eggs 0-2 times/day

Nuts legumes, 1-3 times/day

Alcohol in moderation (if appropiate)

Vegetable (in abundance)

Fruits 2-3 times / day

Whole grain foods (at most meals)

red rice

OATS

Plant oils (olive, canola, soy, corn, sunflower, peanut, and other vegetable oils)

Daily exercise and weight control

# Introduction
# To The Mediterranean Diet Plan

This cookbook is about learning some authentic Mediterranean Diet recipes that fit your budget and meal preps. As to the name of the cookbook, the Mediterranean Diet is all about choosing similar food groups eaten by people living around the Mediterranean Sea.

The Mediterranean Diet is an acclaimed diet plan known to make you lean and healthy and lower the chances of getting any disease.

When you follow a Mediterranean Diet, you live a more active life. With its numerous health benefits discussed in the next portion of this book, the diet incorporates plant-based food and encourages eating vegetables, fruits, whole grains, nuts, beans, and fish. The Oil used to cook meals is usually olive Oil.

The Mediterranean Diet has a lot to offer as it is one of those unique diet plans that are not heavy on budget but also full-filling. So if anyone wants to lose some weight, adopt better eating habits, or regain lost energy, this diet plan is perfect.

When we choose Mediterranean Diet based food groups, we stop feeling unnecessary hunger pangs. The sweet craving is controlled, as the meal's richness makes us feel satisfied. Thus, we do not feel the need to overeat.

In today's fast-paced world, most of us choose unhealthy food because of its accessibility and low cost. Most of us feel frustrated by lengthy cooking procedures and some restrictions that diets offer; well, in the Mediterranean Diet, it's not the case. It is an all-natural diet plan that humans should biologically choose to eat.

The Mediterranean Diet does not offer predefined rules or restrictions, as it is a remarkable way to enjoy life while not depriving oneself of food.

It is not a diet as it is a lifestyle one follows. Well, as a beginner, many of us might be thinking about what food groups are allowed in the diet, why to follow this diet, and what are the benefits of this diet. For the answer, it is necessary to keep reading this cookbook, as it has content that supports the connection between happiness, wellness, and health with Mediterranean Diet.

Now enjoying a flavorful meal and still losing weight is not a problem, as this cookbook introduces 200 recipes with a 28 days Mediterranean Diet meal plan that helps anyone to stay on weight loss track.

Mediterranean Diet is all about mindful eating. While our busy schedules make it hard to prepare meals at home, when we make our meals, we tend to be more linked with our food and well in tune with the cure to our hunger while eating a few calories.

Now, let us start with the basic definition of the Mediterranean Diet.

# Everything You Need to Know
## About Mediterranean Diet

For many of us, the hurdle to our good health and fitness is the word diet, as we feel frustrated by leaving our favorite food items. A person feels restricted and unwilling to follow or even try a new diet plan. The Mediterranean diet is way far different. It is an eating style followed by adopting unique sets of habits in a most exciting and fun way. It is not a choice to make but a lifestyle to follow.

If anyone is obese, or someone fears declining healthy and wants to reduce hunger pangs and make oneself healthy and in better shape, then the Mediterranean diet is the perfect diet plan to follow.

The Mediterranean Diet shows a connection between heart health and longevity. Now, let us look into the basic definition of diet.

## What Is Mediterranean Diet?

The Mediterranean Diet is all about the mindful eating habits of people near the sea. So naturally, the word sea, fresh air, beaches, and some tropical fruits came into one's mind; that is an excellent start to understanding the diet.

In the most straightforward words, the Mediterranean diet is all about choosing and eating healthy, whole, fresh, seasonal, simple, organic, and natural food. The Mediterranean diet is a diverse diet plan that heavily relies on fresh food from all food groups. It's the best diet to enjoy the taste and numerous health benefits.

The Mediterranean coast includes countries like France, Spain, Greece, and Morocco. So while following the Mediterranean Diet, anyone can get the taste of each country's cuisines. Its culinary tradition focused on fresh vegetables, olives, fruits, nuts, olive oil, whole grain, and red wines.

So we can say that the diet is a somewhat diverse cultural adventure that gives the taste buds a roller coaster ride of flavors and respects the family gathering and sharing of food. Listed below are some basics of the diet that help anyone to adopt the diet.

- Mediterranean Diet is about enjoying seasonal, whole, and organic fruits and vegetables. In addition, Mediterranean Diet discourages white flour and encourages incorporating whole wheat flour into the diet.
- Mediterranean Diet encourages nuts and seeds like almonds, walnuts, and cashews.
- If anyone loves butter, start using nuts like walnuts, almonds, and cashews instead of dairy butter.
- Olive Oil is one of the nutritious and healthiest options in the Mediterranean Diet to cook meals or even drizzle over salads.
- Fresh and seasonal spices and herbs are added to a meal to make it more aromatic and rich, with some antioxidant benefits.
- The Mediterranean Diet is all about lean m eat like seas food and chicken.
- Eating pork or red meat is eliminated from the Mediterranean Diet. Still, you can enjoy it once a week.
- It's always advised to use low-fat dairy products.
- Mediterranean Diet highly encourages physical activities; we can t get the benefits from any diet if we are couch potatoes.

## History of the Diet and Science of Eating a Mediterranean Diet

The Mediterranean Diet, by its name, should have been created by the idea that perhaps it is a specific diet consumed by a particular region or country. However, the diet is versatile and based on the seasonal availability of fruits and vegetates. The typical consumption is linked to fruits, olives, and seasonally available vegetables.

Regarding diet history, Dr. Ancel keys were the first person to study diets in 1945.

At that time, the Mediterranean Diet did not get fame or attention. Then in 1958, Dr. Ancel started new research and studied seven countries' diets. While looking at the lifestyle of people and their eating habits, he found that the people living in Mediterranean Diet countries are healthier and have fewer diseases than in other countries. He further noted that the difference in lifestyle and the food incorporated in daily life makes a huge difference.

So, with his further research and study, he found numerous benefits of a diet that led to the Mediterranean diet's success as it started to catch the eye of other countries. Thus till now is a widely recommended and recognized diet and is top among the categories of healthiest diet plans.

## The science behind the Diet for Middle Age Men and Women

The science behind Mediterranean Diet is the focus on healthy fat that other diets restrict. The Mediterranean diet plan suggests that the healthy fats found in nuts and seeds help to remove plaque and fight other diseases. In addition, it helps build a more muscular body and brain.

It also maintains a good sugar level, reduces anxiety and stress, and helps lose weight because of the food choices. In addition, this diet stresses daily physical activity, so the person achieves the best fitness.

# Start Living a Healthy and Happy Life
## by Following a Mediterranean Diet

Whenever we feel our health is declining, we start restricting ourselves from lousy food items. Whatever diet plan we choose to follow comes with benefits; likewise, the Mediterranean Diet is full of benefits that help us start living much healthier and happier. The Mediterranean Diet restricts all dietitians from eating artificial food items, processed food, white sugar, and food rich in carbs. These food groups are the leading cause of hypertension, diabetes, heart-related illness, indigestion, and much more.

Moreover, the lack of physical activity makes the situation even worst. But the Mediterranean Diet encourages physical activity to reap all the benefits of the diet. This diet also helps the body to heal quickly and reduces stress and anxiety. Physical activity also allows us to reduce excess body weight.

Listed below are some health benefits of the Mediterranean Diet.

## Benefits of the Mediterranean Diet

- Because of the healthy food groups added to the diet, the Mediterranean Diet tends to affect the body and mind positively.
- The food choices are dense and make you feel fuller for a longer time, ditching the hunger pangs.
- The diet plan helps you stop sweet cravings and binge eating.
- The vegetables and fruits are rich in multi-nutrients that help fight disease and underlying inflammations.
- The diet helps to reduce stomach-related issues, and the diet incorporates high-fiber food that helps to maintain a healthy gut and digestion.

- Sleep pattern gets better as now we feel less bloated and stressed.
- It initiates effective weight loss.
- It helps in reducing the risk of a heart attack.
- It lower and control hypertension and harmful cholesterol levels.
- It improves brain functions and cognitive skills.
- Less artificial food, carbs, junk, and processed sugar make fewer insulin problems.
- When we lose weight, our self-esteem increases, and we feel much happier.
- When we follow Mediterranean Diet, we tend to eat healthily and start enjoying life.

## Pave your way to a successful weight loss with the Mediterranean Diet

The research and study show that there are millions of people around the world who are overweight and are at risk of cardiovascular diseases. Many of us are so busy in life that we find it hard to reaming healthy. Staying fit while having an active lifestyle or a desk job gets unachievable .while drinking and overeating, and ignoring physical activities make anyone overweight. As the weight increase, the energy reduction makes it impossible to kick start a weight loss journey. Thus the dream of a lean body stays just a dream for many of us.

The good news is that following a Mediterranean diet plan is achievable by remaining fit and feeling energetic while having a lean body. Removing all the processes and junk food is the first step to healthy you. In addition, the Mediterranean diet lowers the lousy fat and increases heart health, thus leading to a slimmer.

## Critical Factors of Obesity and Overweight

Stress and worries related to family, career, job, finances, and health changes hormonal levels and decline in libido. As we age, our muscles weaken, and unnecessary fatigue makes us less involved in physical activities. When we are not physically active, our metabolism rate gets slower. Thus, we become overweight, which leads to several other health issues.

1. So the solution and successful weight are through Mediterranean Diet that focuses on good eating habits while addressing all those issues discussed earlier.

## How Mediterranean Diet Helps in Weight Loss

The Mediterranean diet is rich in fiber and antioxidants that help flush toxins out of the body and slow digestion, thus fewer hunger pangs. In addition, the Mediterranean diet eliminates red meat, refined grains, and processed food. Thus we are already reducing the chances of fat stored in our body.

As Mediterranean Diet is full of nutrients, our muscle becomes stronger; thus, we feel motivated to start an exercise regime already encouraged in Mediterranean Diet.

Food is the central part that helps us reduce weight, but when it is combined with plenty of physical activity, the issue of obesity goes. Mediterranean Diet is about sitting down and enjoying the incredible food that positively affects our mind, and weight loss is a solid mental game. That all sums up nicely how a Mediterranean Diet helps in weight loss.

**CHAPTER NO 3**

# Kick Start the benefits of the
# **Mediterranean Diet Journey**

The most challenging part of a diet plan is how to follow it correctly to gain all its benefits. When eating on Mediterranean Diet, the budget, time, eating habits, and family food preferences should be kept in mind. To kick start the Mediterranean Diet journey, you need to do the following:

- Switch the cooking oil with olive Oil.
- Remove all the junk food from the pantry, like sodas, candies, and packed food items.
- Buy vegetables and fruits that are seasonal.
- Cook a fresh meal at home.
- Replace white flour with whole wheat flour.
- White rice should be replaced by brown rice.
- When buying any store-bought item, read the food labels carefully for any hidden sugar.
- Don't be bored and change the menu daily.

## Planning the Mediterranean Diet

1. We recommend planning the Mediterranean Diet that fits everyone's daily food intake as we do not encourage the reader to not starve on this diet plan, nor does this diet serve this purpose. The diet may feel challenging for some people as it demands changing their budget, medical needs, time, and eating preferences. To better adapt to the Mediterranean Diet plan, here are some guidelines. Therefore, we provide guidelines that help any person plan and incorporate the diet into their daily routine.

## Guidelines

- Always start the meal by filling the half plate with seasonal fruits and vegetables, for which salad choices are a great option.

- Appreciate the choices and make a list of food that your family members prefer to eat.
- Avoid artificial favoring, processed food, and sugar.
- Adjust the time to eat the meal and follow the set protocol every day.
- Try eating breakfast as early as possible once you wake up.
- Emphasis should be on fish, fruits, vegetables, whole-wheat grains, and chicken.
- Prepare a weekly list of food to purchase so food does not get wasted.
- Do not dump any leftover food, as it's an excellent option to prepare the specific serving when anyone wants to eat.
- Buy new food once the fridge is getting empty.
- The grocery list should include seafood, fruits, chicken, and low-fat dairy items.

The meal plan is a thoughtful and time taking process, so to help all the reader to kick start the journey, we have introduced 7 day sample meal plan, 200 recipes, and 28 days complete meal plan to choose from efficiently.

## Tips for Success

- Make fruits and vegetables a staple of your daily diet.
- Limit the homemade fresh juice intake to ½ cup per day.
- The lunch should incorporate a bowl of salads or simple fruits.
- Replace white flour with whole grain flour.
- Replace the white rice with brown rice.
- Eliminate the process and refined grains and use faro, millet, oats, barley, whole wheat pasta, couscous, and plenty as a central part of your diet.
- Choose low-fat dairy items.
- Choose low-fat milk, Greek yogurt, and cheese.

- Eat fish rich in omega 3.
- The fish is recommended to be eaten twice a week.
- Drink wine in moderation, about 5-8 ounces per day.
- Use healthy protein and fat options, like nuts, seeds, and cheese.
- Snack on nuts.
- Reduce the consumption of pork and red meat; if you like red meat, it's allowed to be consumed once a week.
- Cut off the salt intake and replace it with spices and herbs like garlic to make the dish savory.
- Do not use processed white sugar.
- Add sweetness to the meal or dessert in honey or brown sugar.
- Stop being a couch potato, have some movement into your daily routine.
- If you do not like going to the gym, make sure to walk or jog daily and have a home-based workout routine.
- Avoid canned food items.
- A balanced diet is one way to start the diet successfully.
- The healthiest beverages in Mediterranean Diet are coffee (no added sugar), water, green tea, low-fat milk, and fruit smooth with 1% of milk fat).

## CHAPTER NO 4

# Eating
# On Mediterranean Diet

The Mediterranean diet offers nutritious food choices with beautiful vistas, as we know that only healthy, whole, and organic food are part of this diet, making it a hit diet.

Listed below is the shopping guide while following Mediterranean Diet.

## Shopping Guide:

Food allowed daily includes:

- Organic and seasonal vegetables (carrots, broccoli, kale, garlic, spinach, kale)
- Olive Oil
- Organic and seasonal fresh fruits
- Nut oils
- Whole grains
- Whole wheat
- Seeds
- Nuts
- Beans
- Legumes (check for your allergies)
- Herbs
- Spices
- Low-fat dairy products

## Food Allowed All Week

- Fish
- Chicken
- Eggs
- Cheese
- Greek Yogurt
- Seafood

## Food to Eat Once A Week

- Red meat
- Sweet treats (use brown sugar or honey)

## Food Not Allowed

- White Sugar
- White rice
- White flour
- Junk food
- Deep fried food
- Canned and Sweetened beverages
- Added Sugars
- Processed meat
- Refined grains
- Refined Oil for cooking
- Processed food items
- Packed food items

## Healthy Snacks allowed

- Handful of nuts
- Bowl of Fruits (organic and fresh)
- Bowl of Vegetables like carrots
- Greek Yogurt or a few slices of cheese
- Almond butter
- Peanut butter (look if you have allergies)
- A handful of mixed Berrie's
- Cucumber
- Green leafy vegetable salad
- Soft cheese
- Nuts Milk
- Chickpeas
- Olives

## Eating Out On Mediterranean Diet

Eating out is a must, and we cannot avoid it, as our friends and families often invite us for celebrations and dinners.

If you love to eat out, you can choose your meal on the Mediterranean Diet's premises.

- As a starter, choose a vegetarian entry and plant-based sources of protein.
- When eating out, we seldom know which Oil is used for cooking the meal, so avoid dishes made of Oil and choose baked and grilled items like grilled fish and grilled or roasted chicken.
- 6-8 ounces of wine is an excellent option if planning to drink.
- Always order salads made with fresh green leafy vegetables to fill your plate.
- Mexican food is an excellent fit for Mediterranean Diet, as it includes brown rice, corn tortilla, lettuce, and salsa, fajita vegetables that are amazingly mouthwatering and good to go.

## 7 days sample menu plan

### Day 1

Breakfast : Greek yogurt topped with walnuts and 2 banana chunks.
Lunch : lentil soup with whole grain bread
Dinner : hummus with pita bread and grilled vegetables

### Day 2

Breakfast : vegetable frittata
Lunch : salmon and brown rice Buddha bowl
Dinner : baked fish with garlic sauce

### Day 3

Breakfast : Greek yogurt parfait
Lunch : Mediterranean shrimp
Dinner : roasted potatoes and baked fish fillet

### Day 4

Breakfast : green smoothie
Lunch : tuna salad
Dinner : grilled chicken with vegetables

### Day 5

Breakfast : steel-cut oats topped with nuts and fruits
Lunch : chickpea and farro salad
Dinner : Mediterranean pasta

### Day 6

Breakfast : shakshuka
Lunch : shrimp-based whole wheat pasta
Dinner : roasted chicken with vegetables

### Day 7

Breakfast : chia pudding
Lunch : chickpea soup
Dinner : balsamic roasted chicken with a fresh vegetable salad

Now let's start with the part of the recipe.

**RECIPE NOTE :** Recipes are tagged with GF and DF, where DF is dairy-free, and GF is gluten-free.

# 21 Breakfast Recipes

## 1. Strawberry-Thyme Millet Bowl (GF and DF)

 **Prep Time:** 20 Minutes |  **Cook Time:** 25 Minutes |  **Serves:** 2

### Ingredients

- 1 pound of strawberries, halved
- 2 sprigs of fresh thyme
- 1 tablespoon of olive oil
- 2 teaspoons of maple syrup
- 1 cup almond milk
- 1 cup millet
- 1 cup water
- 1 teaspoon vanilla extract
- 2 teaspoons of pistachios
- 2 teaspoons almonds
- 1 teaspoon hemp seeds

1.

### Directions

2. Preheat the oven to 400 degrees F.
3. Line a parchment paper inside a baking sheet, or grease it with oil spray.
4. Add strawberries, oil, thyme, and maple syrup to a bowl and add it to a baking sheet.
5. Bake it inside the preheated oven for about 22 minutes.
6. Next, take a cooking pot and pour milk into it.
7. Pour water and bring to a perfect boil.
8. Add in the millet and cook, covered for 25 minutes with low heat.
9. Add in the vanilla once the water and almond milk are absorbed.
10. Once done, top the millet with oven-baked berries and its juices collected on a baking sheet.
11. Top it with hemp seed, almonds, and pistachios.
12. Enjoy.

## 2. Migas (GF)

 **Prep Time:** 15 Minutes |  **Cook Time:** 15 Minutes |  **Serves:** 3

### Ingredients

- 4 tablespoons olive oil
- 14 small corn tortillas
- 2 jalapenos
- 2 cloves of garlic
- 6 eggs
- 1/3 cup feta cheese
- 1/3 cup chopped cilantro

- Salt and black pepper to taste
- 1 cup cooked Black beans (pre-cooked)
- 1 large organic Avocados, or as per liking
- ½ cup of homemade Tomato salsa or more

## Directions

1. Heat 1 tablespoon of olive oil in a large skillet.
2. Add tortillas to the skillet and fry from both sides until done.
3. Set the tortillas aside.
4. Add remaining olive oil to the skillet and cook jalapeno and garlic for a few minutes.
5. Crack eggs into the skillet and cook the eggs until firm.
6. Now, top it off with the herbs like cilantro and add feta cheese on top.
7. Now, distribute the eggs between the tortillas and top with black beans, avocado, and salsa.
8. Enjoy a delicious breakfast.

## 3. Sandwiches Filled With Egg, Cheese, Spinach, and Tomato

|  Prep Time: 10 Minutes |  Cook Time: 10 Minutes |  Serves: 1 |
|---|---|---|

### Ingredients

- 2 multigrain sandwich thins
- 2 teaspoons olive oil
- 1/2 teaspoon rosemary, dry and crushed
- 2 organic eggs
- 1 cup of baby spinach leaves
- ½ medium tomatoes cut into slices
- 3-4 tablespoons feta cheese, crumbled and reduced-fat
- Salt and black pepper to taste

### Directions

1. First, preheat the oven to 400 degrees F.
2. Brush one side of both the bread slices with olive oil
3. Now toast it in preheated oven at 400 degrees F for a few minutes.
4. Once slightly toasted, take it out.
5. Heat the remaining olive oil in a cooking pan, add rosemary, and cook eggs in the skillet for 1 minute.
6. Season the egg with salt and black pepper.

7. Cook the yolk according to personal preference.
8. Once done, remove it from the heat.
9. Place the egg on the bread slice and layer the spinach, feta cheese, and tomatoes.
10. Top with the remaining bread slice and make a sandwich.
11. Serve and enjoy.

## 4. Vegetable Scrambled Eggs (GF)

|  Prep Time: 10 Minutes |  Cook Time: 8 Minutes |  Serves: 2 |
|---|---|---|

### Ingredients

- 2 tablespoons olive oil
- ½ chopped green bell peppers
- ½ red tomatoes, chopped
- Salt and black pepper to taste
- ½ teaspoon paprika
- 4 organic eggs, whisked
- 1/6 teaspoon red pepper flakes, just a few pinches
- 2 black olive, chopped
- ¼ cup cilantro, fresh and chopped
- ¼ cup of parsley, chopped

### Directions

1. Take a skillet and pour olive oil into it.
2. Add green bell pepper and cook until slightly wilted.
3. Add in the tomatoes and let them cook for 1 minute.
4. Now season veggies with salt, pepper, and paprika, and add olives
5. Stir it twice and crack eggs into the skillet
6. Cook until eggs get firm.
7. Top with fresh herbs like parsley and cilantro.
8. Sprinkle red chili flakes on top.
9. Adjust the seasoning and serve with whole wheat bread.

## 5. Brioche Bread (GF)

|  Prep Time: 16 Minutes |  Cook Time: 25-30 Minutes |  Serves: 4 |
|---|---|---|

### Ingredients

- 2 Cups of Low-Fat dairy milk
- 1/3 cup brown sugar
- 2 tablespoons yeast
- 4-1/4 cups flour
- 4-6 organic eggs

- 1 tablespoon vanilla extract
- 1 cup light olive oil butter
- 1 egg, whisked for coating

## Directions

1. In a large bowl, pour milk.
2. Add to the milk the dry yeast, eggs, and sugar.
3. Whisk it well.
4. Then add the flour.
5. Make dough of the mixture and knead the dough onto a flat surface.
6. Leave it for 1 hour until it gets double in size.
7. Knit the dough several times.
8. Make rolls out of the dough and apply the egg wash over the rolls while arranging them onto a baking sheet lined with parchment paper or greased with oil spray.
9. Bake it in the oven for 25-30 minutes at 350 degrees F.
10. Once done, serve.

## 6. Cheesy Mushrooms and Egg Tartine

|  Prep Time: 12 Minutes |  Cook Time: 15 Minutes |  Serves: 2 |
| --- | --- | --- |

### Ingredients

- 4 whole wheat bread slices
- 2 teaspoons of Olive oil, divided
- 1 cup ricotta cheese
- 2 tablespoons plant-based butter
- 4 cloves garlic, chopped
- 2 cups mixed mushrooms
- 2 tablespoons sherry vinegar
- Salt and black pepper to taste
- 1/3 cup chopped walnuts
- 4 organic eggs
- ½ tablespoon chopped chilies
- 2 teaspoons of Dill
- 2 teaspoons of Basil leaves

### Directions

1. Toast the bread slices in the toaster until done.
2. Set them aside.
3. Take a skillet and add butter to it.
4. Let it get melt, and add olive oil as well.
5. Cook the garlic in it until aroma comes.
6. Then add mushrooms and cook for 4 minutes.
7. Season the skillet mixture with salt, black pepper, and vinegar.
8. Add in the walnuts and cook for 2 minutes
9. Set this mixture aside.
10. Now in a small frying pan, heat a few drops of oil and fry the eggs as you like.
11. Take a toast and layering it with mushroom mixture, eggs, and ricotta.
12. Top with another slice.
13. Make two sandwiches like that.
14. Serve and enjoy.

## 7. Blueberries Bowl

|  Prep Time: 5 Minutes |  Cook Time: 20 Minutes | Serves: 1-2 |
| --- | --- | --- |

### Ingredients

- 2 cups of frozen blueberries
- 1/3 cup of unsweetened almond milk
- 4 tablespoons of almond butter, unsweetened
- 1/4 cup granola
- Toppings:
- 2 teaspoons of sliced almonds
- 2 teaspoons of hemp seeds

### Directions

1. Take a high-speed blender and add blueberries, almond milk, butter, and granola.
2. Pulse it into a puree.
3. Transfer it to a bowl and top with sliced almonds and hemp seeds.
4. Enjoy.

## 8. Sunny-Side-Up Eggs on Garlicky Greens (GF)

|  Prep Time: 12 Minutes |  Cook Time: 10-12 Minutes |  Serves: 3 |
| --- | --- | --- |

## Ingredients

- 2 tablespoons olive oil, divided
- 2 cups mixed greens
- 4 garlic cloves, minced
- 1 cup grape tomatoes
- 4-6 eggs, whisked
- Salt and black pepper to taste

## Directions

1. Heat half of the olive oil in a cooking pan and cook the garlic in the pan until the aroma comes.
2. Add the green to it for a few minutes.
3. Now add grape tomatoes and let it cook for 1 minute
4. Transfer it to a serving plate.
5. Add more olive oil to the skillet and cook the eggs sunny.
6. Season the eggs with salt and black pepper.
7. Serve the eggs over the greens.
8. Enjoy

# 9. Nectarine Bruschetta (GF)

 **Prep Time:** 15 Minutes   **Cook Time:** 2 Minutes   **Serves:** 2

## Ingredients

- 2 tablespoons red wine vinegar
- 2 teaspoons brown sugar
- 2 nectarines
- 1/2 cup olive oil
- 2 teaspoons black pepper
- 1/3 cup fresh ricotta cheese
- 4 whole wheat bread slices

## Directions

1. In a large bowl, combine brown sugar and red wine vinegar.
2. Whisk it well.
3. Now add the nectarine.
4. Toss well.
5. Season it with pepper and olive oil.
6. Now toast the bread in a toaster.
7. Top the bread slices with nectarine mixture and top with ricotta.
8. Serve and enjoy.

# 10. Spinach Crepes with Apples and Chickpeas (GF)

 **Prep Time:** 40 Minutes   **Cook Time:** 25 -30 Minutes   **Serves:** 4-6

## Ingredients

- 4 organic eggs
- ½ cup cilantro, chopped
- Black pepper, to taste
- 2-1/2 cup of low-fat milk
- 1 cup whole wheat flour+2 tablespoons of additional flour
- 3 tablespoons of olive oil, divided
- Salt, to taste
- 1 yellow onion, chopped
- 14 ounces of chickpeas, rinsed and drained
- 2 granny smith apples, diced
- 1/4 cup golden raisins
- 4 teaspoons of madras curry powder
- 2 cups fresh spinach
- Few Lemon wedges for serving

## Directions

1. Take a high-speed blender to add eggs and season it with pepper, cilantro, and 1 cup of milk.
2. Now add 2 tablespoons of oil.
3. Then add the 1 cup of flour.
4. Then add in the salt.
5. Make a batter.
6. Lightly grease a skillet with oil spray.
7. Pour 1/3 cup batter and cook until edges are cooked.
8. Flip to cook for 30 seconds.
9. Cook the crepes until all the batter is consumed.
10. Cover all the crepes until warm.
11. Heat oil in skillet and cook onion.
12. Add chickpeas, raisins, curry powder, and apples.
13. Cook for 4 minutes.
14. Add 2 tablespoons of the remaining flour.
15. Stir the remaining ingredients.
16. Add in the spinach.
17. Cook until wilted.
18. Divide it amongst the crepes and fold.
19. Serve with lemon wedges if liked.

# 11. Mediterranean Homemade Croissant

 **Preparation Time:** 25 Minutes   **Cooking Time:** 20 Minutes   **Servings:** 2-4

## Ingredients

- 2 cups whole wheat flour
- ½ cup brown sugar
- 2 teaspoons yeast

- Salt, pinch
- 1 cup light olive oil butter
- 1 cup milk, or as needed
- 1 cup Egg washes mixture for coating

## Directions

1. Combine flour, sugar, yeast, and salt in a bowl.
2. In a separate bowl, whisk eggs to prepare an egg wash.
3. Now into the flour, add butter, and mix in the butter with the flour
4. Then add milk and make dough out of the batter.
5. Let the dough sit in the refrigerator for a few hours.
6. Next, roll the dough onto a flat surface.
7. Cut the dough into rectangles.
8. Fold the rectangles six to seven times.
9. Put the croissant onto a baking sheet lined with parchment paper.
10. Add it to the oven and bake for 20 minutes at 365 degrees F.
11. Once the croissants are ready, serve and enjoy.

# 12. Breakfast Pogaca

 **Preparation Time:** 25 Minutes   **Cooking Time:** 30 Minutes   **Servings:** 6

## Ingredients

- For dough:
- 3-1/2 cups whole wheat flour
- 1/2 cup warm milk
- 1 tablespoon of yeast
- ½ cup olive oil
- 1 tablespoon sugar
- 1/6 teaspoon salt
- 2 cups water
- For Filling:
- Handful of Parsley
- 2 cups feta cheese, crumbled
- For Topping:
- 2 egg yolks, whisked and for coating
- A few tablespoons of Poppy seeds

## Directions

1. Combine the sugar, flour, olive oil, salt, yeast, and milk in a bowl.
2. Mix well and set aside.
3. Add a little bit of water as well.

4. Let the mixture rest for a while so the yeast does its action.
5. In a separate bowl, combine cheese with parsley.
6. After 1 hour, the dough will be double its size.
7. Divide the dough into equal size balls and then roll them to flatten it.
8. Once the dough is flattening, add the cheese mixture into the middle of the dough.
9. Now fold the dough to make small balls.
10. Now line a baking sheet with parchment paper.
11. Add the dough balls to the baking sheet.
12. Brush it with egg yolk wash, and drizzle poppy seeds on top.
13. Add the baking sheet to the oven.
14. Bake it in the oven for 30 minutes at 250 degrees F.
15. Once it's done, serve.

# 13. Goat Cheese Egg Muffins with Spinach (GF)

 **Preparation Time:** 20 Minutes  **Cooking Time:** 25-30 Minutes   **Servings:** 2

## Ingredients

- 1 tablespoon olive oil
- Cooking spray for greasing
- ½ teaspoon of red peppers
- Salt and black pepper to taste
- 2 scallions, peeled and chopped
- 6 eggs, whisked
- ¼ cup almond milk
- 16 ounces of baby spinach
- ½ cup goat cheese

## Directions

1. Preheat the oven to 350 degrees F.
2. Grease the muffin tray with cooking spray or line it with muffin paper cups.
3. Heat oil in a skillet and let it get warm.
4. Cook the scallions in it.
5. Then add red pepper, salt, and black pepper.
6. Now put in the spinach and let it cook until wilted.
7. Transfer the spinach to a large bowl.
8. Now crack eggs in a bowl once spinach cools off.
9. Pour in the almond milk and whisk the eggs well.
10. Now pour the egg mixture into the muffin tray.
11. Top the egg muffins equally with cheese crumbles.

12. Add it to the oven and bake it for 25- 30 minutes at 350 degrees F.
13. Once the muffins are ready, let them relax and serve.
14. Enjoy.

# 14. Breakfast Creamy Avocado Omelets (GF)

 **Preparation Time:** 15 Minutes |  **Cooking Time:** 8-10 Minutes |  **Servings:** 3

## Ingredients

- ½ teaspoon olive oil
- ½ small onion, chopped
- Salt and black pepper to taste
- 6 cremini mushrooms
- ½ cup baby spinach
- ¼ cup broccoli florets, chopped
- 6 medium eggs
- 2 ounces of shredded mozzarella cheese
- ½ cup grape tomatoes
- 1/6 cup parsley
- ½ medium avocados

## Directions

1. Heat oil in a skillet and cook onions in it.
2. Sauté the onions for a few minutes until translucent
3. Then add salt and black pepper to it
4. Next, add the mushrooms and cook the mushrooms for 5 minutes.
5. Now add the spinach along with mushrooms and broccoli florets, and let it cook for 1 minute.
6. Now crack eggs in a separate bowl and whisk them well.
7. Pour the eggs over the skillet mixture.
8. Cook the omelet until firm; just before taking out the omelet, add cheese over the top.
9. Let it cook for a minute more, then serve with parsley, grape tomatoes, and avocado slices.

# 15. Tomato and Egg Stacks (GF and DF)

 **Preparation Time:** 15 Minutes |  **Cooking Time:** 25-30 Minutes |  **Servings:** 2

## Ingredients

- 2 teaspoons olive oil
- 1 onion, chopped
- 2 teaspoons fresh thyme
- Salt and black pepper to taste
- 2 beefsteak tomato, sliced
- 6-ounce shredded mozzarella cheese
- 6 slices of eggplants
- 4 eggs, whisked

## Directions

1. Preheat the oven to 370 degrees F.
2. Heat oil to the skillet and cook onions in it for a few minutes,
3. Then add the thyme and season the onion with salt and black pepper.
4. Take a baking pan and grease it with cooking spray.
5. Stack the tomato slices onto the bottom of the pan.
6. Top the slices with cheese and cooked onions from the skillet.
7. Pour on top the whisked eggs.
8. Add the baking pan to the oven and cook for 22-25 minutes at 350 degrees F.
9. Meanwhile, grill eggplants on a preheated grill or bake them in the oven alongside eggs.
10. Then serve the eggplants over the stack of Egg and tomatoes.
11. Adjust the seasoning and serve.

# 16. Avocado Smoothie (GF and DF)

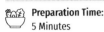 **Preparation Time:** 5 Minutes    **Cooking Time:** 0 Minutes    **Servings:** 4

## Ingredients

- 2 avocados pitted
- 4 bananas, frozen
- ½ cup spinach
- 1 cup almond milk
- 6 Medjool dates, pitted

## Directions

1. Put all the listed ingredients in a blender.
2. Blend it until smooth.
3. Pour it into tall ice-filled serving glasses.
4. Enjoy a healthy breakfast smoothie option that keeps you full all day long.

# 17. Butternut Squash and Spinach Toast

 **Preparation Time:** 15 Minutes    **Cooking Time:** 20 Minutes    **Servings:** 4

## Ingredients

- 1 butternut squash, peeled, chopped, and seedless
- 1 tablespoon olive oil+1/2 teaspoons of olive oil
- 2 garlic cloves, chopped
- 1 cup baby spinach
- Salt and black pepper to taste
- 4 bread slices, whole wheat, and organic
- 1/2 cup feta cheese
- 4 eggs, fried

## Directions

1. Peel and chop the butternut squash.
2. Cut into pieces and discard the seeds.
3. Take a skillet and add olive oil to it.
4. Then sauté the garlic until the aroma comes.
5. Cook the squash for 12 minutes with the lid on top, so it gets soft and tender.
6. Then add salt and pepper to season the squash.
7. Now toast the whole wheat bread slices in the toaster.
8. Fry eggs in a small frying pan by adding additional olive oil.
9. Layer the bread with cooked squash, fried eggs, cheese, and baby spinach.

# 18. Shakshuka (GF)

 **Preparation Time:** 20 Minutes    **Cooking Time:** 25-30 Minutes    **Servings:** 4

## Ingredients

- 2 tablespoons olive oil
- 1 tablespoon onion, chopped
- 2 red bell peppers, chopped
- 4 cloves garlic, chopped
- 2cups of crushed tomatoes
- 1 cup of tomatoes, diced
- 2 tablespoons harissa
- ½ teaspoons cumin
- ½ teaspoon paprika
- ½ teaspoon coriander
- ¼ teaspoon red pepper flakes
- Salt and freshly ground black pepper to taste
- 8 eggs, whisked
- 1 cup crumbled feta
- Few parsley leaves, as needed
- 4 whole wheat bread slices

## Directions

1. Preheat the oven to 400 degrees F.
2. Heat oil in a skillet and cook onions for a few minutes.
3. Once the onions get caramelized, add garlic.
4. Let it cook until the aroma comes.
5. Cook it for 1 minute and add harissa, salt, black pepper, crushed and diced tomato, and spices
6. Cook it until soft.
7. Transfer this prepared skillet mixture into the oil-greased baking pan.
8. Make 8 holes in the baking pan mixture.
9. Pour one egg into each hole and then pour the Egg into the sauce.
10. Season the eggs with salt and black pepper.
11. Cover the baking pan with foil.
12. Let it bake for 16 minutes.
13. Once done, serve with a topping of cheese and a sprinkle of parsley.
14. Serve with pita bread.
15. Enjoy.

# 19. Sweet Potato and Spinach Frittata (GF)

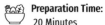

## Ingredients

- 6 medium eggs
- 1 cup of coconut cream
- Salt and freshly ground black pepper to taste
- 2 cups sweet potatoes, shredded
- 2 tablespoons olive oil
- 1 cup spinach, chopped
- 1 red onion, peeled and chopped
- 4 garlic cloves, minced
- 4-ounce Feta cheese

## Directions

1. Preheat the oven to 350 degrees F for a few minutes.
2. Take a bowl and whisk eggs in it
3. Then add coconut cream to it
4. Season it with salt and black pepper.
5. Whisk it again.
6. Now, heat oil in a skillet and cook sweet potatoes at medium flame for 12 minutes; stir occasionally.
7. Next, add spinach, garlic, and red onions
8. Let it cook for 3 more minutes
9. Now add the whisked eggs to a skillet and cook for 3 minutes
10. Then top it with cheese and bake it in the oven at 320 degrees F until the cheese melt.
11. Once baked, serve and enjoy.

## 20. Easy Savory Oatmeal Bowls

 **Preparation Time:**
25 Minutes

 **Cooking Time:**
20 Minutes

 **Servings:**
2

## Ingredients

- 2 small yellow onions, chopped
- 2 sweet potatoes, peeled and chopped
- Salt and black pepper to taste
- 1 cup steel-cut oats
- 6 eggs
- 1 large avocado, cut into small cubes
- 1-1/2 cup cherry tomatoes, halved
- 1cup chopped fresh parsley

- ½ cup of Feta cheese, crumbled
- Zapata, as needed
- 2-3 tablespoons of olive oil

## Directions

1. Take a skillet and heat 2 tablespoons of olive oil in it.
2. Cook sweet potatoes in it for a few minutes.
3. Season the sweet potatoes with salt and black pepper.
4. Cover the sweet potatoes with a lid and cook for 10 minutes until soft and tender.
5. Meanwhile, cook the oats in 2 cups of water until done.
6. Season the oats with salt and black pepper.
7. Fry the eggs in a separate frying pan using the remaining olive oil.
8. Now assemble the breakfast bowl by adding oats, topping off with eggs and sweet potatoes, and serving it with avocado slices, avatar, cherry tomato, cheese, and parsley.
9. Add some additional seasoning, as liked.
10. Enjoy.

## 21. Blueberry-And-Mixed Nut Parfait (GF)

 **Preparation Time:**
25 Minutes

 **Cooking Time:**
20 Minutes

 **Servings:**
4

## Ingredients

- 2-1/2 cups blueberries, frozen
- 2 cups water
- 6 tablespoons walnuts
- 6 tablespoons almonds
- 4 tablespoons pecans
- 4 tablespoons Pepitas
- Oil spray for misting or greasing
- ½ teaspoon cinnamon
- 1/3 teaspoon cardamom
- Sea salt, to taste
- 1-2 tablespoons orange zest
- 1/3 cup golden raisins
- 4 cups Greek yogurt

## Directions

1. Take a high-speed food processor and add frozen blueberries to it.

2. Pulse it until powder.
3. Take a cooking pot and pour water into it.
4. Add a pinch of salt as well.
5. Cook for 10 minutes until thick.
6.  Meanwhile, layer Pepitas, walnuts, almonds, and pea cans on a baking sheet.
7. Add a pinch of cinnamon and cardamom to it as well.
8. Remember to mist the nuts with oil spray.
9. Bake the nuts in the oven at 390 degrees F for 8 minutes.
10. Add the zest of orange and raisins to the blueberries
11. Cook it for a minute
12. Now add geek yogurt to the serving bowl, top with blueberry sauce, and add baked nuts on top.
13. Enjoy

# CHAPTER NO 6

# 20 Vegetables and Bean

## 1. Baked Eggplant with Tomatoes and Feta Cheese (GF)

 **Preparation Time:** 20 Minutes |  **Cooking Time:** 35 Minutes |  **Servings:** 2

### Ingredients

- 4 eggplants cut lengthwise
- 2 tablespoons of Olive oil
- 6 ounces of Feta cheese
- The tomato sauce:
- 1/3 cup olive oil
- 4 garlic cloves
- 16 ounces of tomatoes (chopped)
- Few Basil leaves
- Salt and black pepper to taste
- 2 tablespoons balsamic vinegar
- 2 teaspoons of brown sugar

### Directions

1. Preheat the oven to around 390 degrees F, coat the eggplants with olive oil, sprinkle some salt, and put them on a baking tray.
2. Place the baking tray in the oven and cook the eggplants for around 25 minutes or till they become soft and tender.
3. Meanwhile, heat olive oil in a large pan and cook garlic in it.
4. Once fragrant, chop and add tomatoes, seasoning it with salt, pepper, and herbs and let it simmer for 15 minutes.
5. Then take it off the heat, take out the herb springs and mix in sugar and balsamic vinegar.
6. Pour the tomato sauce over the aubergines, sprinkle some feta cheese, and bake until the tomato starts bubbling.

# 2. Tortilla Espanola (GF)

 **Preparation Time:**
12 Minutes

 **Cooking Time:**
15 Minutes

**Servings:**
2

## Ingredients

- ¼ cup olive oil
- 1 pound potatoes
- 1 white onion
- 6 eggs
- 1/2 teaspoons salt

## Directions

1. Start by heating oil in a skillet over medium heat and add potatoes and onions once hot.
2. Cook both of them for around 10 minutes.
3. While cooking, crack and beat all the eggs with salt in a bowl.
4. Pour the eggs into the skillet and place the skillet in the oven, broiling it for 5 minutes.
5. When done, give it a sprinkle of salt and serve.

# 3. Garlic Parmesan White Beans (GF)

**Preparation Time:**
15 Minutes

**Cooking Time:**
25 Minutes

**Servings:**
3

## Ingredients

- 4 garlic cloves, minced
- 3 teaspoons of extra virgin olive oil
- 14 ounces of cannellini beans, cooked
- 1 cup cherry tomatoes, halved
- Salt and black pepper
- 2 teaspoons Aleppo pepper
- ½ teaspoon cumin
- 1 cup chopped fresh parsley
- ¼ to ⅓ cup shaved Parmesan cheese
- ¼ cup grated Pecorino Romano
- Juice half a lemon
- Side: pita bread

## Directions

1. Heat 2 tablespoons extra virgin olive oil in a pan and cook garlic until golden brown.
2. Then mix in the pan in cannellini beans, ½ cup of water, salt, tomatoes, black pepper, and spices.
3. Cook them for around 10 minutes or till it is warmed.
4. Next, mix in parsley, cheese, and lemon juice.

5. Give a drizzle of extra virgin olive oil and serve with the side of pita or bread.

# 4. Mediterranean Chickpea Stew with Spinach & Feta (GF)

 **Preparation Time:**
15 Minutes

 **Cooking Time:**
25 Minutes

 **Servings:**
3

## Ingredients

- 1 tablespoon olive oil
- 4 small red onions
- 4cloves garlic
- 1 teaspoon dried oregano
- ½ teaspoon cayenne powder
- 1/4 teaspoon cloves powder
- 15 ounces chopped tomatoes
- 1 cup vegetable stock
- 1 tablespoon balsamic vinegar
- 15-ounce chickpeas
- 3 cups spinach
- 6 ounces feta
- Salt and black pepper to taste

## Directions

1. Heat the oil in a skillet and sauté the onions for 5 minutes.
2. Then mix in garlic, oregano, cayenne, and cloves, cooking them for another 2 minutes.
3. Then add stock, vinegar, and tomatoes and cook until the sauce thickens.
4. Once it's thickened, mix in feta cheese, spinach, and chickpeas, cooking it for another 3 minutes.
5. Season with salt and pepper, and serve with a garnish of parsley.

# 5. Roasted Vegan Greek Lemon Potatoes (GF and DF)

 **Preparation Time:**
20 Minutes

 **Cooking Time:**
60 Minutes

 **Servings:**
2

## Ingredients

- 2.4 pounds of russet potatoes (peeled, quartered lengthwise)
- 2 cups vegetable broth (low sodium)
- ½ cup white wine
- 2 tablespoons lemon juice
- 1/2 teaspoon garlic powder
- 1 teaspoon oregano
- 1 teaspoon rosemary
- Sea salt, to taste
- 1 -1/4 tablespoon corn starch
- Lemon wedges, as needed

## Directions

1. Preheat the oven to around 425 degrees F.
2. Quarter the potatoes and arrange them on the baking dish in an even layer.
3. Mix all the remaining listed ingredients in a bowl and add them to the quartered potatoes.
4. Place a foil or parchment paper over the potatoes and cook them for 30 to 40 minutes or until they are tender.
5. When done, take off the foil and toss the potatoes with sauce, cooking for another 20 minutes or till the liquid is dissolved.

## 6. Eggplant Dip (GF and DF)

 **Preparation Time:** 20 Minutes |  **Cooking Time:** 15 Minutes |  **Servings:** 2

## Ingredients

- 4 small eggplants
- 2 garlic cloves
- 4 tablespoons tahini
- 1 lemon juice only
- 3 tablespoons olive oil
- 1 teaspoon paprika
- Salt and Pepper to taste
- Garnish
- 1 tablespoon pomegranate seeds
- 2tablespoons cilantro

## Directions

1. Begin by heating the oven to 350 degrees F.
2. Coat the eggplants with oil and season them with some salt.
3. Use a fork and make some holes in the skin of the eggplants.
4. Arrange the eggplants with the garlic in the baking dish and roast them till they become tender.
5. Once tender, slice the eggplant in half, and take out the flesh.
6. Shift the eggplant to the food processor and process them with all the remaining listed ingredients.
7. Shift the Ganoush to the bowl, serve with a drizzle of olive oil, and garnish with cilantro and pomegranate seeds.

## 7. Radish Tzatziki (GF)

 **Preparation Time:** 10 Minutes |  **Cooking Time:** 0 Minutes |  **Servings:** 4

## Ingredients

- 2.5 cups Greek yogurt
- 1 cup radishes
- 1/2 cup toasted walnuts
- 4 tablespoons dill (chopped)
- 2 tablespoons olive oil
- 2 tablespoons lemon juice
- Salt and black pepper to taste

## Directions

1. Start by mixing radishes, dill, yogurt, walnuts, olive oil, lemon juice, black pepper, and salt in a bowl till everything is mixed thoroughly.
2. Once mixed, serve it with a side of sliced vegetables, or it can be placed in the fridge for later use.

## 8. Lentil and Greens Salad with Feta and Pear (GF)

 **Preparation Time:** 15 Minutes |  **Cooking Time:** 0 Minutes |  **Servings:** 2

## Ingredients

- 1 cup lentils, cooked
- 4 cups spinach
- 2 sliced pear s
- Handful of walnuts
- For the Dressing
- 2 teaspoons honey
- 2 teaspoons mustard
- 1 tablespoon balsamic vinegar
- ¼ cup olive oil
- Salt and black pepper to taste

## Directions

1. Start by adding all the ingredients for the dressing in a bowl and give them a mix.
2. In another bowl, add the lentils and give them a mix with salad dressing.
3. Next, mix the greens and sliced pears and top it with walnuts and cheese.

# 9. Curry Broccoli and Cauliflower (GF)

 **Preparation Time:** 20 Minutes  **Cooking Time:** 35-45 Minutes  **Servings:** 2

## Ingredients

- 1 broccoli head, chopped
- ½ cauliflower head, chopped
- 1 cup parmesan cheese, grated
- ½ cup sun-dried tomatoes in oil
- 7 garlic cloves (diced finely)
- 3 tablespoon olive oil
- ½ teaspoon curry powder

## Directions

1. Begin by preheating the oven to around 390 degrees F.
2. Add olive oil, cheese, sundried tomatoes, garlic, cheese, and curry powder to a bowl and mix them.
3. Slice the cauliflower and broccoli head into florets and add them to the bowl, giving them a mix and evenly coating them.
4. Shift everything to a baking dish and cover it using foil.
5. Place the baking dish in the oven and let them cook for around 20 minutes.
6. Take the foil off and stir everything so they are cooked throughout.

7. Once tossed, cover the baking dish with the foil again and bake it for another 10 to 15 minutes or till they are nice and brown.
8. When done, season accordingly with salt and pepper and serve.

# 10. Beans and Greens with Polenta

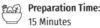 **Preparation Time:** 15 Minutes  **Cooking Time:** 55-60 Minutes  **Servings:** 4

## Ingredients

- 1 cup olive oil
- 1 onion, chopped
- 1/2 cup parsley
- 1/2 cup dill
- 2 cups Swiss chard
- 3 cans of black-eyed peas
- 1 tablespoon tomato paste
- 1 lemon juice
- Salt and pepper
- Ingredients for Polenta
- 5 cups vegetable broth
- 1-1/4 cup cornmeal
- 2 garlic cloves
- 1/3 cup coconut milk
- 2 tablespoons olive oil
- Salt and black pepper to taste

## Directions

1. Start by heating olive oil in a saucepan over medium heat.
2. Once hot, add onions to it and sauté them for 2 minutes.
3. Then mix in Swiss chard, dill, and parsley, and cook them for 5 more minutes.
4. Once the chard is wilted, mix in beans, lemon juice, tomato paste, and seasoning according to taste.
5. Let it cook for around 30 minutes.
6. While cooking, add broth to a separate pot, mix in cornmeal, and let it cook for 15 minutes.
7. Once it's thickened, mix in milk, garlic, oil, salt, and pepper.
8. Once everything is cooked, serve the polenta with the greens and beans on the side.

# 11. Tomato Shakshuka (GF and DF)

 **Preparation Time:** 20 Minutes    30 Minutes    **Servings:** 2    **Cooking Time:**

## Ingredients

- 3 teaspoons olive oil
- 2 onions, diced
- 1 can of diced tomatoes
- 4 small red tomatoes, chopped
- 2 tablespoons tomato paste
- 2 s red chilies
- 4 eggs
- Handful parsley
- 1 teaspoon paprika
- Salt and black pepper to taste

## Directions

1. First, preheat the oven to around 320 degrees F.
2. Heat oil in a frying pan and add onions, sautéing them till they are soft and browned.
3. Once the onions are done, mix in diced tomato can, tomato paste, and tomatoes.
4. Simmer them for 10 minutes and season them with salt, pepper, oregano, and paprika according to taste.
5. Cook the tomatoes for a few more minutes and shift them to a heatproof dish.
6. Use the back of the spoon and make two indents, cracking eggs in them and placing it in the oven, cooking them for around 8 to 10 minutes.
7. When done, serve with a garnish of parsley and a side of brown rice or wholegrain bread.

## 12. White Bean Hummus (GF and DF)

 **Preparation Time:** 5 Minutes |  **Cooking Time:** 0 Minutes |  **Servings:** 4

## Ingredients

- 12 ounces of cannellini beans
- 2 ounces shallots
- 4 tablespoons olive oil, divided
- 4 tablespoons lemon juice
- 1/2 teaspoon garlic
- 1 teaspoon cumin powder
- 1 teaspoon coriander powder
- 1 teaspoon thyme leaves
- Salt, to taste
- 1/3 teaspoon cayenne pepper
- 2 teaspoons sweet paprika

## Directions

1. Add all the listed ingredients except the paprika to a food blender and blend them till a smooth consistency is achieved.
2. Once it's smooth, shift the hummus into a bowl.
3. In another bowl, mix oil and paprika and serve on the side with the hummus.

## 13. Gnocchi and Brussels sprouts (GF and DF)

 **Preparation Time:** 20 Minutes |  **Cooking Time:** 20 Minutes |  **Servings:** 4

## Ingredients

- 1-2 Meyer lemons
- 1 pound Brussels sprout (trimmed, quartered)
- 14 ounces package gnocchi
- ½ cup shallots, sliced
- 4 tablespoons olive oil
- Salt and black pepper to taste
- ½ cup sun-dried tomatoes, oil-packed

## Directions

1. Preheat the oven to around 450 degrees F.
2. Add 2 tablespoons of oil, Brussels sprouts, gnocchi, and shallots to a bowl.
3. Season it with salt and pepper according to taste and squeeze the lemons over it.
4. Toss everything to coat evenly.
5. Shift the vegetables to a baking dish and place them in the oven, roasting them for 18 to 20 minutes. Make sure to stir the vegetables at least two times while cooking to ensure an even cook throughout.
6. Toss gnocchi with lemon juice and mix it with sun-dried tomatoes, oil and salt, and pepper according to taste.

## 14. Falafel with Tahini (GF and DF)

 **Preparation Time:** 15 Minutes |  **Cooking Time:** 25 Minutes |  **Servings:** 4

## Ingredients

- ½ cup tahini
- 2 teaspoons lemon juice
- Sea salt, to taste
- 3 cups cooked chickpeas
- 1 onion
- 5 garlic cloves
- 1 teaspoon red chili flakes
- 1 teaspoon cumin
- 1 teaspoon baking powder
- 1/2 cup almond flour
- 1/4 cup parsley
- 1/4 cup cilantro
- 1 cup olive oil for cooking

## Directions

1. Add tahini, garlic, lemon juice, and salt to a bowl and mix them.
2. Add chickpeas, onions, garlic, chili flakes, cumin, flour, cilantro, parsley, and baking powder in a food blender and blend everything till a smooth consistency is achieved.
3. Keep the mixture in the fridge for a few hours to cool down.
4. Scoop the batter and make circles with it.
5. Heat oil in a skillet and cook the falafel circles until crispy.
6. When done, serve the falafel with the side of tahini.

# 15. Mediterranean Spinach & Beans (GF and DF)

|  Preparation Time:<br>15 Minutes |  Cooking Time:<br>20-22 Minutes |  Servings:<br>2 |
|---|---|---|

## Ingredients

- 2 tablespoons olive oil and more
- 1 small onion, chopped
- 2 garlic cloves, minced
- 1 cup tomatoes, diced
- 2 tablespoons Worcestershire sauce
- Salt and black pepper to taste
- 1/4 teaspoon crushed red pepper flakes
- 14 ounces of cannellini beans, rinsed and drained
- 14 ounces of artichoke hearts, water-packed, quartered
- 8 cups of baby spinach

## Directions

1. Add oil to a 12-inch skillet and heat it over medium heat, sautéing the onions once hot.
2. Cook the onions for around 3 to 5 minutes and mix in garlic, cooking for another minute.
3. Once the fragrant, mix in tomatoes, Worcestershire sauce, and all the seasonings.
4. Bring everything to a boil, reducing the heat and letting it simmer for 6 to 8 minutes without a lid.
5. Once all the water is almost evaporated, mix beans, artichoke hearts, and spinach, cooking it for 3 to 5 minutes or till wilted.
6. Give it a drizzle of olive oil if desired, and serve.

# 16. Seasoned Haricot Beans (GF and DF)

|  Preparation Time:<br>20 Minutes |  Cooking Time:<br>3 Hours 10 Mins |  Servings:<br>3 |
|---|---|---|

## Ingredients

- 1 pound of dried haricot beans, dried
- 4 tablespoons olive oil
- 1 clove of garlic, minced
- 1 bay leaf
- 1 onion, chopped
- 3 cloves garlic, minced
- 1 large tomato, chopped
- 1 red bell pepper, chopped
- 1 teaspoon cayenne flakes, to taste
- 4 large sage leaves
- 1 sprig of rosemary
- Water to cover and for soaking
- Salt and black pepper to taste
- A handful of chives, chopped

## Directions

1. Start by soaking beans in a pot of water and let it soak for at least 6 hours or overnight.
2. Once soaked, drain the chickpeas and shift them to a pot of fresh water at least 2 inches deep.
3. Give a splash of olive oil, place in a bay leaf and garlic, and bring it to a boil.
4. Once it begins to boil, lower the heat and let it simmer with a lid for 1 ½ hour.
5. Make sure the beans are tender before mixing in the seasoning.

6. In another pan, cook the onions with olive oil.
7. Once the onions are soft, mix in bell pepper and tomatoes.
8. Cook them for a few minutes, and then add garlic, pepper, sage, rosemary, cayenne, black pepper, and salt.
9. Mix everything and cook it for another 5 minutes over low heat.
10. After that, shift the vegetables and herbs into a pot and cook it with seasoning for ½ hour, stirring after some time.
11. Once done, garnish with some chives and serve.

# 17. Greek Chickpea Stew (GF and DF)

| Preparation Time: 20 Minutes | Cooking Time: 3 Hours 10 Minutes | Servings: 3 |
|---|---|---|

## Ingredients

- 1-1/2 cups dry chickpeas
- 1-1/2 cup water
- 2 onions, diced
- 2 garlic cloves
- 1 bay leaf
- ¼ cup olive oil
- Salt and black pepper
- Lemon wedges, as needed

## Directions

1. Mix onions, garlic, bay leaf, oil, and salt in a pot and let it cook for around 5 minutes.
2. After 5 minutes, mix chickpeas and pour water to submerge everything.
3. Cook the beans for around 3 hours or till soft.
4. Give a drizzle of oil, lemon juice, and pepper, and serve.

# 18. Roasted White Beans with Vegetables Greek Style (GF)

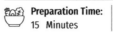  

| Preparation Time: 15 Minutes | Cooking Time: 70 Minutes | Servings: 4 |
|---|---|---|

## Ingredients

- 2.5 cups white beans
- 1/3 cup olive oil
- ½ red bell peppers
- ½ green bell pepper
- 2 small onions
- 4 garlic cloves
- 10 cherry tomatoes
- ½ tablespoon oregano
- 2 tablespoons tomato paste
- Salt and black pepper to taste
- ½ cup cheese, or as needed

## Directions

1. Start by soaking the white beans in a water bowl for at least overnight.
2. Once soaked, shift the beans into a pot and cook it for around 30 minutes over low heat.
3. Meanwhile, preheat the oven to around 346 degrees F.
4. Chop the vegetables and shift them to a bowl.
5. Mix tomato paste, onions, garlic, oregano, pepper, and oil with the vegetables.
6. Then toss cherry tomatoes in the bowl and shift it to a casserole dish.
7. Pour in a bit of water, add beans and cover it with foil.
8. Place the dish in the oven and cook it for around 40 minutes.
9. Once browned, serve it with some seasoning and a garnish of cheese.

# 19. Greek Roasted Chickpeas (GF and DF)

 **Preparation Time:**
20 Minutes

 **Cooking Time:**
75 Minutes

**Servings:**
2

## Ingredients

- 1 cup chickpeas
- 1 onion, chopped
- 2 garlic cloves
- 1 bay leaf
- 1 tablespoon tomato paste
- 2 tablespoons dill
- 2 tablespoons olive oil
- Salt and black pepper to taste

## Directions

1. Start by soaking chickpeas for at least 8 hours or overnight.
2. Add onions, garlic, beans, bay leaves, and chickpeas to a pot of water, and cook it for 45 minutes over low heat.
3. Once cooked, drain them and set them aside.
4. Meanwhile, preheat them to 360 degrees F.
5. Next, mix tomato paste with the beans and shift it into the casserole dish.
6. Give a drizzle of oil and sprinkle some dill over the dish.
7. Season with some salt and pepper, and pour a bit of water into the dish.
8. Cover the dish with foil, place it in the oven, and cook it for around 30 minutes.
9. When browned, take it out and serve.

# 20. Pan Con Tomato (DF)

 **Preparation Time:**
10 Minutes

 **Cooking Time:**
2 Minutes

**Servings:**
2

## Ingredients

- 1 loaf of ciabatta bread, sliced
- 4 garlic cloves
- 1-2 grated tomatoes
- 4 tablespoons olive oil
- Black pepper and sea salt, to taste

## Directions

1. Start by slicing the bread into 6 pieces and arranging them on the baking dish.
2. Dice tomatoes in a bowl and set aside.
3. Place the bread in a broiler and cook it for around 2 minutes.
4. Add the diced tomatoes and garlic cloves to the bread when toasted.
5. Toast the bread with olive oil and season with some sea salt.
6. When done, serve and enjoy.

**CHAPTER NO 7**

# 29 Pasta, Rice, Pies

## 1. Helen's Mediterranean Pie

 **Preparation Time:** 25 Minutes |  **Cooking Time:** 60 Minutes |  **Servings:** 2

### Ingredients

- 2 pounds of potatoes
- 1 cup milk
- 1 small onion
- ½ red peppers
- 1 courgette
- 3 tablespoons olive oil
- 2 cloves of garlic
- 2 teaspoons bouillon powder, optional
- 2 cups chickpeas, drained
- 2 cups chopped tomatoes
- 1 teaspoon dried mixed herbs
- 2 tablespoons of sunflower seeds

### Directions

1. Start by cleaning and dicing the potatoes.
2. Add them to a pot of boiling water and cook it for around 15 minutes or till softened.
3. Once soft, drain them and mash them, mixing them with milk.
4. Chop the onions, slice the pepper, trim and dice the courgette, and set aside.
5. Heat oil on medium heat and add onions and crushed garlic once hot.
6. Then mix in bouillon powder and fry everything for around 5 minutes.
7. Next, add pepper and courgette to the pot and mix them.
8. Drain the chickpeas and shift them in the pot, mixing them with tomatoes and dried herbs.
9. Then bring everything to a boil and reduce the heat once it begins to boil, letting it simmer for around 10 minutes.
10. Shift everything into a 25x30cm dish and add the mashed potato.
11. Use a fork and create a texture over it.
12. Sprinkle some sunflower seeds on top and place them in the oven.
13. Cook them for 25 to 30 minutes at 350 degrees F and serve.

# 2. Greek Spinach Pies

 **Preparation Time:** 20 Minutes |  **Cooking Time:** 30 Minutes | **Servings:** 2

## Ingredients:

- ½ cup salted butter, plant-based
- 2/3 cup onions (diced)
- 4 cups spinach leaves
- 12 sheets of filo dough
- 1 cup of feta cheese, crumbled
- ½ cup ricotta cheese
- 1 egg yolk
- 1 tablespoon lemon juice
- 1 teaspoon dill, chopped
- ½ teaspoon garlic powder
- Salt, to taste

## Directions

1. Begin by preheating the oven to around 375 degrees F.
2. Heat oil in a skillet and sauté onions in it once the oil is hot.
3. Sauté the onions till they are translucent.
4. Once soft and translucent, mix in spinach and let it cook till wilted.
5. Mix spinach, feta cheese, ricotta cheese, salt, onions, lemon juice, dill, and garlic powder in a bowl.
6. Arrange Phyllo dough on a clean, flat surface, lightly brushing it with oil.
7. Place dough on the surface and brush more oil over that dough.
8. Slice the dough into 1/3rd and add 1 ½ tablespoon filling in each slice.
9. Fold the dough from the bottom, keeping the triangle shape intact.
10. Brush egg washes on the dough and sprinkles some sesame seeds on top.
11. Arrange them on the baking dish and cook them in the preheated oven till crispy and golden brown.

# 3. Mediterranean Pie (GF)

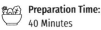 **Preparation Time:** 40 Minutes |  **Cooking Time:** 80 Minutes |  **Servings:** 2

## Ingredients

- 2 tablespoons plant-based butter
- 2 sweet red peppers, diced
- 4 small onions, chopped
- 4 garlic cloves, minced
- 12 ounces frozen spinach, thawed & squeezed dry (I use my ricer)
- 12 ounces of frozen puff pastry, thawed
- 10 ounces of black forest ham, sliced
- 1 pound of mozzarella cheese, grated
- 10 eggs, beaten & seasoned with
- Salt and black pepper to taste
- Egg whisked (for glaze)

## Directions

1. Start by melting butter in a skillet and cook pepper, garlic, and onions for around 12 minutes or until there is no liquid.
2. Once done, take it off the heat, mix in spinach, and set aside.
3. Roll the pastry till 1/8 inch thick.
4. Please place it in the pan and let some extra dough drape over the edge.
5. Layer ham, half of the cheese, and half of the vegetables in the pan, covering it with the pastry, trimming the edges, and brushing egg wash over it.
6. Place the pan in an oven preheated to around 400 degrees F and cook it for about 15 minutes.
7. After 15 minutes, reduce the heat to 350 and let it cook for 45 to 60 minutes or till the top of the pastry is crispy, golden brown, and cooked from the center.
8. When done, take the pastry out, let it rest for at least 15 minutes, and serve.

# 4. Classic Mediterranean Pie

 **Preparation Time:** 20 Minutes |  **Cooking Time:** 30-35 Minutes |  **Servings:** 2

## Ingredients

- 1 sheet puff pastry, thawed
- ½ cup of feta cheese, crumbled
- 8 cherry tomatoes halved
- 1 small zucchini, thinly sliced
- 6 slices of salami quartered
- 1/2 cup pitted black olives
- 1 cup of Baby rocket leaves to serve

## Directions

1. Start by preheating the oven to around 200 degrees C.
2. Add some baking paper to the bottom of the baking dish.
3. Slice the corner of puff pastry to form a round shape and place it in the prepared dish.
4. Mix feta cheese, zucchini, salami, olives, cherry tomatoes, and seasoning in a bowl.
5. Shift the mixture into the pastry, leaving at least a 4 cm border on the corner.
6. Raise the edges around the filling and keep the center open.
7. Place it in the preheated oven and cook it for 30 to 35 minutes or till the pastry is crispy and golden brown.
8. Serve the pie with a garnish of baby rocket leaves.

## 5. Chicken Pie

 **Preparation Time:** 25 Minutes |  **Cooking Time:** 20-30 Minutes |  **Servings:** 3

### Ingredients

- 2 tablespoons coconut oil
- 4 tablespoons plain whole wheat flour
- 2 cups semi-skimmed milk
- 3 cups chicken stock
- 5-6 sheets of filo pastry
- Oil spray for greasing
- 1 teaspoon of paprika, sweet smoked
- 1 pound of cooked skinless chicken breasts
- 1 cup grilled vegetables in oil
- 1 cup of mixed olives and feta
- Oregano sprigs leave picked
- Lemon juice to taste
- Lemon wedges, to serve

### Directions

1. Start by heating an oven to around 200 degrees F.
2. Mix butter, flour, milk, and stock in a saucepan and heat it over medium heat for 10 minutes. Make sure to mix till the sauce is thick constantly.
3. Place the Phyllo dough in a baking dish and sprinkle with oil and a pinch of paprika.
4. Place them in the oven and cook them for 10 minutes or till crispy and golden brown.
5. Use 2 forks and shred the chicken breasts.

6. Once the béchamel sauce is thickened, mix in ½ teaspoon paprika, shredded chicken, char grilled vegetables, feta cheese, olive oil, and oregano.
7. Season with salt, pepper, and lemon juice according to taste and cook it till boiling.
8. Top a piece of crispy filo with the filling and serve it with the side of lemon wedges or lemon juice.

## 6. Mediterranean Meat Pies

 **Preparation Time:** 15 Minutes |  **Cooking Time:** 40 Minutes |  **Servings:** 2-4

### Ingredients

- 2 pounds of ground beef
- 1 pound ground lamb
- 2 white onions, finely chopped
- 1/2 cup pine nuts
- 1/6 teaspoon ground cinnamon
- Salt and black pepper to taste
- ⅓ cup lemon juice
- 22 ounces of frozen puff pastry, thawed
- 2 eggs, beaten

### Directions

1. Add ground beef, ground lamb, onion, pine nuts, cinnamon, salt, and black pepper in a skillet over medium heat and mix everything.
2. Cook the meat till it is browned, crumbled and is no pinker.
3. Remove the extra grease and mix in lemon juice, adjust the taste with salt and pepper, and let it cool down.
4. Heat the oven to around 350 degrees F.
5. Grease the bottom of a baking dish or place parchment paper over it.
6. Place the thawed pastry sheet on a flat surface and roll it till 1/8 inch thick.
7. Cut out nine 3-inch rounds using a cookie cutter and coat the inside edges with water.
8. Fill the center of the dough with 2 tablespoons of the filling and fold the pastry in half, covering the filling and closing the edges.
9. Shift the pastries into a baking dish and place it in the oven, cooking it for 15 to 20 minutes or till golden brown.

# 7. Cauliflower Tapas

 **Preparation Time:** 15 Minutes | **Cooking Time:** 25 Minutes | **Servings:** 2-4

## Ingredients

- 1 Cauliflower head, chopped
- Oil, as needed for frying
- 6 eggs
- 2 cups bread crumbs
- 1 teaspoon paprika
- Salt, to taste

## Directions

1. Chop the cauliflower head into florets and add them to a pot of boiling water.
2. When soft, take the florets out and drain the water.
3. While the cauliflower is boiling, add the florets to a skillet with vegetable oil and cook them over medium heat.
4. Crack and whisk together eggs in a bowl.
5. In another bowl, mix breadcrumbs and paprika powder.
6. Take the florets, dip them in the eggs, and then give them a coat of breadcrumbs.
7. Add the cauliflower florets in oil and fry them till golden brown.
8. Take them out, season with salt and pepper, and serve.

# 8. Lemony Mediterranean Rice (GF)

 **Preparation Time:** 20 Minutes | **Cooking Time:** 22 Minutes | **Servings:** 2

## Ingredients

- 2 tablespoons olive oil
- 1 onion, sliced
- 2 garlic cloves, chopped
- 1 teaspoon oregano, dried
- 1 cup rice
- 1 cup chickpea, cooked
- 3 cups vegetable stock
- 2 lemons zest and juice
- 2 tablespoons dill (fresh)
- 4 ounces feta cheese (crumbled)

- Salt and black pepper, to taste

## Directions

1. Heat olive oil in a pressure cooker and sauté onions in it.
2. Once the onions are soft, mix in oregano and rice and stir until the rice begins to turn translucent.
3. Then pour the stock, chickpeas, lemon juice, and zest into the pot, season with salt and pepper, and cook them on high pressure for 6 minutes.
4. Then release the pressure and let everything simmer for 15 minutes.
5. Once all the water has evaporated, mix in dill and feta cheese and serve.

# 9. Chickpeas and Rice with Tahini (DF)

 **Preparation Time:** 25 Minutes |  **Cooking Time:** 70 Minutes |  **Servings:** 2

## Ingredients

- 2 cups chickpeas
- 2 teaspoons of tahini
- 2 lemon juice
- 2 teaspoons of extra virgin olive oil
- 1 onion, chopped
- 1 garlic clove, chopped
- ½ cup uncooked rice
- Salt and black pepper, to taste
- 2 bay leaves
- A handful of Parsley leaves, chopped

## Directions

1. Start by letting the chickpeas soak in water for at least 8 hours.
2. Then shift them into a pot and cook them for 40 minutes.
3. Heat oils over medium heat in a pot and sautés the onions.
4. Mix tahini, water, and lemon juice in a bowl.
5. When the onions are cooked, add garlic, chickpeas, and rice with it.
6. Pour the tahini sauce over the rice, season with salt and pepper, and pour 2 cups water into it.
7. Cook everything for 20 minutes and serve with a sprinkle of parsley.

# 10. One Pot Pasta

 **Preparation Time:** 25 Minutes |  **Cooking Time:** 15 Minutes |  **Servings:** 4

## Ingredients

- 12 ounces whole wheat pasta
- 4 cups chopped kale
- 2 cups of tomatoes
- 2 chopped onions
- 6 garlic cloves
- 2 tablespoons pesto
- 2 teaspoons of Italian seasoning
- Salt and black pepper, to taste
- 4 cups water
- Garnish
- Pesto, as needed
- 1 cup Parmesan cheese

## Directions

1. Combine garlic, pasta, kale pasta, kale, tomatoes, onion, Italian seasoning, salt, black pepper, and crushed red pepper along with 4 cups of water in a pot.
2. Let it simmer, and cover it with a lid.
3. Cook it for 15 minutes.
4. Once it's cooked, garnish with cheese and pesto.
5. Serve and enjoy!

# 11. Chicken Parmesan Pasta

 **Preparation Time:** 22 Minutes |  **Cooking Time:** 25 Minutes |  **Servings:** 2-4

## Ingredients

- 4 teaspoons of olive oil, divided
- 1/3 cup Panko breadcrumbs
- 1 teaspoon of crushed garlic
- 1 pound chicken breast, cubed
- 1 teaspoon of Italian seasoning
- 4 cups chicken broth
- 2.5 cups tomatoes
- 12 ounces whole wheat pasta
- 1/2 cup mozzarella cheese
- ½ cup Parmesan cheese
- ½ cup fresh basil
- Salt and black pepper to taste

## Directions

1. Heat oil in a skillet and cook Panko bread crumbs for 2 minutes.
2. Then add garlic and cook until aroma comes.
3. Transfer this into a separate bowl.
4. Add some more oil into the pan, add chicken, and let it cook until it turns brown.
5. Then add salt, pepper, and Italian seasoning.
6. Pour in the broth and pasta along with tomatoes.
7. Let it cook with the lid on top for 20 minutes.
8. Then top it with both listed kinds of cheese.
9. Preheat the broiler.
10. Add the pasta pan to the oven and broil until the cheese melts.
11. Serve with the garnish of basil.
12.

# 12. Bruschetta Pasta

 **Preparation Time:** 25 Minutes |  **Cooking Time:** 2-25 Minutes |  **Servings:** 2

## Ingredients

- 6 ounces whole wheat spaghetti
- 2 tablespoons of olive oil
- 1.5 pounds of chicken breasts
- 1 tablespoon or less Italian seasoning
- 1.5 pints cherry tomatoes
- 6 garlic cloves
- Salt and black pepper to taste
- 1 tablespoon of balsamic vinegar
- 1 cup of Parmesan cheese
- 1/3 cup basil leaves, chopped

## Directions

1. Cook pasta according to package instructions.
2. Take a cooking pan and heat the oil in it.
3. Add chicken to it and let it cook until it gets brown.
4. Sprinkle the Italian seasoning, salt, and pepper on the cooking pan and cook for 5 minutes.
5. Then transfer it to the plate.
6. Now add tomatoes and garlic and cook for 5 more minutes.
7. Add the balsamic vinegar as well.
8. Put the cooked pasta into the pot.
9. Cook it for a few minutes, then serve with a sprinkle of cheese and basil leaves.

# 13. One-Pot Greek Pasta

 **Preparation Time:**
20 Minutes

 **Cooking Time:**
5-10 Minutes

**Servings:**
2

## Ingredients

- 4 teaspoons of olive oil
- 1 pound of chicken sausage
- 1 cup of onion, diced
- 2 garlic cloves, crushed
- 2 cups of tomato sauce
- 2 cups baby spinach
- 6 ounces whole wheat pasta, cooked
- ¼ cup Kalamata olives, chopped
- 1cup feta cheese

## Directions

1. Heat olive oil in a skillet.
2. Cook the onions and garlic until the aroma comes.
3. Then add tomato sauce, and chicken sausage, and let it cook for 5 minutes.
4. Then add the spinach, olives, and cooked pasta,
5. Cover it with the lid.
6. Let it cook for 5 more minutes.
7. Once vegetables get wilted, add a few teaspoons of water.
8. Add the cheese at the end and serve.
9. Enjoy!
10.

# 14. Greek Spaghetti

 **Preparation Time:**
25 Minutes

 **Cooking Time:**
55-60 Minutes

**Servings:**
4

## Ingredients

- 4 cup crushed tomatoes
- 2 pounds lamb
- 1 small onion, chopped
- 4 cloves garlic
- 1 cup red wine
- 1 cup water
- 1 teaspoon allspice powder
- Salt and black pepper to taste
- 22 ounces spaghetti

- 2 tablespoons of olive oil
- 1 cup of feta cheese

## Directions

1. Pour the oil into a large cooking pan or pot.
2. Cook the onions in it for 2 minutes.
3. Then cook lamb and let it cook for 10 minutes.
4. Add garlic and cook until garlic gives an aroma.
5. Next, pour the wine, tomatoes and their juice, allspice powder, salt, water, and black pepper.
6. Let it cook with the lid on top for about 55 minutes.
7. Till then, the sauce gets thick.
8. Meanwhile, cook whole wheat spaghetti in a pan according to package instructions.
9. Serve meat over spaghetti with a topping of feta cheese.
10. Serve and enjoy.
11.

# 15. Creamy Pasta with Broccoli and Mushrooms

 **Preparation Time:**
20 Minutes

 **Cooking Time:**
30-35 Minutes

 **Servings:**
2

## Ingredients

- 10 ounces fettuccine, whole wheat
- 1 tablespoon of extra-virgin olive oil
- 3 cups sliced mushrooms
- 3 cups broccoli, florets
- 1 tablespoon crushed garlic
- 1/2 cup red wine
- 2 cups milk
- 2tablespoons of whole wheat flour
- Salt and black pepper, to taste
- 1 cup Asiago cheese, shredded

## Directions

1. Cook the pasta according to package instructions.
2. Heat olive oil in a large skillet, and put the garlic in it.
3. Cook the garlic for 2 minutes, then add the mushrooms and sauté mushrooms.
4. Cook it for 2 minutes, then add broccoli.
5. Let it cook just for 3-4 minutes.
6. Season it with salt, pepper, rosemary, and red wine, and bring the mixture to a boil.

7. Combine whole wheat flour, salt, pepper, and almond milk in a bowl.
8. Pour the mixture into the skillet and let it cook for 2 minutes.
9. Once the sauce gets thickened, top it with cheese.
10. Toss it over cooked pasta and serve.
11. Enjoy!

# 16. Chicken Pesto Pasta with Broccoli

 **Preparation Time:** 22 Minutes   **Cooking Time:** 35 Minutes   **Servings:** 2

## Ingredient

- 10 ounces penne, whole wheat
- 2 teaspoons of olive oil
- 1 pound broccoli, floret, and cubed
- 2-3 cups chicken breast, cubed
- 7-ounce basil pesto
- Salt and black pepper, to taste
- ¼ cup Parmesan cheese
- Basil leaves

## Directions

1. Cook the whole wheat pasta in a large pot, according to package instructions.
2. Once it's done, drain the pasta, and reserve some of the liquid.
3. Heat olive oil in a skillet.
4. Cook chicken in the skillet.
5. Add pepper and salt.
6. Then add reserved water and cook the chicken until tender.
7. Add in the broccoli and cook for 3 minutes.
8. Now add pesto.
9. Let it stir a few times, and then serve over cooked pasta with parmesan cheese and basil.
10. Add pasta to skillet and stir well.
11. Once combined, serve.

# 17. Chicken and Kale Pasta with Lemon and Parmesan

 **Preparation Time:** 15 Minutes   22 Minutes   **Servings:** 3   **Cooking Time:**

## Ingredients

- 8 ounces whole wheat pasta
- 2 tablespoons of olive oil
- 1.5 pounds boneless, skinless chicken breast
- Salt and black pepper to taste
- 4 crushed garlic
- ½ cup red wine
- 1 tablespoon of lemon juice
- 4 cups spinach
- 6 tablespoons of Parmesan cheese

## Directions

1. Cook pasta according to package instructions.
2. Then drain and set aside for further use.
3. Heat oil in a skillet and cook chicken, salt, and black pepper.
4. Then add garlic and cook for 5 minutes.
5. Now add red wine along with lemon juice and lemon zest.
6. Let it boil.
7. Then add the spinach and cooked drained pasta.
8. Cook for 4 minutes and serve and enjoy with a sprinkle of parmesan cheese.
9.

# 18. Ravioli with Arugula & Pecorino

 **Preparation Time:** 18 Minutes   **Cooking Time:** 22 Minutes   **Servings:** 2

## Ingredients

- 1 pound cheese ravioli, fresh and whole-wheat
- 2 cloves of garlic, minced
- Salt and black pepper to taste
- ¼ cup extra-virgin olive oil
- 2 large shallots, sliced
- 2 tablespoons red-wine vinegar
- 2 teaspoons Dijon mustard
- 5 cups arugula
- 1 cup shaved parmesan cheese

## Directions

1. Cook ravioli in boiling water for 7 minutes or according to package instructions.
2. Drain and set it aside.

3. Next, heat olive oil in a skillet and add garlic, black pepper, and salt.
4. Then add shallots and cook the shallots for 3 minutes.
5. Then add vinegar, mustard, and black pepper.
6. Toss cooked ravioli with arugula and add it to the skillet
7. Let it cook for 1 minute.
8. Serve it with parmesan cheese.
9.

# 19. Simple Mediterranean Olive Oil Pasta

 **Preparation Time:** 15 Minutes   **Cooking Time:** 22 Minutes   **Servings:** 2

## Ingredients

- 1 pound of whole wheat spaghetti
- 1/3 cup olive oil
- 4 garlic cloves, crushed
- Salt and black pepper to taste
- 12 ounces of grape tomatoes, halved
- 2 scallions, peeled and chopped
- 7 ounces of marinated artichoke hearts, drained
- 1/3 cup pitted olives, halved
- 1/3 cup crumbled feta cheese, more if you like
- 8 fresh basil leaves, torn
- 1 lemon, juice, and zest
- Crushed red pepper flakes, optional

## Directions

1. Cook the pasta according to package instructions.
2. Remember to add olive oil and salt to the water once cooking pasta.
3. Drain and set it aside once done.
4. Next, heat oil in a skillet, cook garlic and stir in parsley.
5. Add tomatoes, scallion, artichokes, and olives, and cook over low heat for 1 minute.
6. Serve it over cooked pasta with a topping of lemon, red crushed pepper flakes, olives, lemon juice, lemon zest, and feta cheese.
7. Enjoy with a topping of basil leaves.

# 20. Orange and Cranberry Rice

 **Preparation Time:** 20 Minutes   **Cooking Time:** 35 Minutes   **Servings:** 4

## Ingredients

- 2 cups rice pilaf
- 2 teaspoons of olive oil
- 1 cup water
- 2 cups chicken stock with crushed pieces
- ½ teaspoon of coconut sugar
- Salt, to taste
- 1 teaspoon of curry powder
- 1/2 cup cranberries
- 3 scallions
- 1/3 cup parsley
- 12/2 orange zest

## Directions

1. Take a cooking pan and add olive oil to it.
2. Then add sugar, salt, water, and chicken stock.
3. Let it simmer for 5 minutes.
4. Then add rice, curry powder, cranberry, and orange zest.
5. Let it simmer until the liquid evaporates.
6. Then cover it with a lid and cook for 25 minutes.
7. Once the rice gets fluffy and cooked, serve with a topping of parsley and scallions.
8. Enjoy.

# 21. Greek Rice Pilaf

 **Preparation Time:** 25 Minutes   **Cooking Time:** 20 Minutes   **Servings:** 2

## Ingredients

- 1 small onion, peeled and chopped
- 2 teaspoons of olive oil
- 2 garlic cloves, minced
- 2 tablespoons of mint
- Salt and black pepper, to taste
- 3 cups spinach
- 4 teaspoons of lemon juice
- 4 cups cooked rice
- 1 cup green peas
- 2 tablespoons of dill
- 1 cup feta cheese

## Directions

1. Heat oil in a skillet and add onions for cooking.
2. Once the onions get soft, add garlic, pepper, and mint, and cook for 2 minutes.
3. Next, add dill, peas, and spinach

4. Let the spinach get soft
5. Now add the rice and lemon juice.
6. Add the cooked rice and cover it with a lid
7. Stir it well before covering
8. Let it cook for 5 minutes.
9. Afterward, garnish the rice with feta cheese.
10. Enjoy!
11.

## 22. Simple Coconut Rice (DF)

 **Preparation Time:** 15 Minutes |  **Cooking Time:** 25 Minutes |  **Servings:** 4

### Ingredients

- 1.5 cups jasmine rice, presoaked
- 1.5 cups Coconut Milk
- 1.5 cups water
- 1 kaffir lime leaf
- Salt, to taste
- 4 tablespoons of flaked coconut

### Directions

1. First, wash the rice and let it soak in water for a few minutes.
2. Take a large pot and pour in the water.
3. Now add a lime leaf, coconut milk, and salt and bring it to a boil.
4. Once the boil comes, add the rice and stir well
5. Let cook until liquid evaporates
6. Then cover it with a lid and cook for 20 minutes
7. Garnish with roasted coconut flakes and serve.
8. Enjoy!

## 23. Autumn Chestnut Rice (DF)

 **Preparation Time:** 20 Minutes |  **Cooking Time:** 25 Minutes |  **Servings:** 4

### Ingredients

- 2 cups Long grain rice
- 4 cups water
- 4 leeks
- 1/2 cup chestnuts
- ¼ cup cilantro
- Salt, to taste

### Directions

1. Take a large pot and boil water in it.
2. Then add presoaked and drained rice.
3. Let it simmer until water evaporates.
4. Add salt and add leeks and chestnuts.
5. Once water simmers down, cover and cook the rice for 20 minutes
6. Then serve and enjoy with a topping of cilantro.

## 24. Rice with Butternut Casserole

 **Preparation Time:** 22 Minutes |  **Cooking Time:** 35 Minutes |  **Servings:** 4

### Ingredients

- Oil spray for greasing
- 1 cup wild rice
- 2 tablespoons olive oil
- Salt and black pepper to taste
- ½ butternut squash, diced
- 1 onion rough chopped
- 2 tablespoons thyme
- 2 teaspoons dried sage
- 1 teaspoon dried marjoram
- 3/4 cup cranberries
- 1/3 cup pecans
- 1/3 cup Parmesan cheese

### Directions

1. Preheat the oven to 420 degrees F.
2. Grease a baking sheet with oil spray.
3. Cook the rice according to package instructions.
4. Season the squash with oil, salt, and pepper.
5. Put the squash in a baking tray and bake in the oven until golden and tender.
6. Now add onions onto the baking pan and cook for 5 minutes.
7. Add olive oil, cranberries, listed herbs, pecans, salt, and black pepper to the cooked baking tray ingredients.
8. Add in the rice, onion, and squash.
9. Spread all this mixture into a casserole dish and top with cheese
10. Bake in the oven for 10 minutes.
11. Serve and enjoy!

## 25. Lemony Rice with Feta

# Cheese

 **Preparation Time:** 45 Minutes |  **Cooking Time:** 30 Minutes |  **Servings:** 2

## Ingredients

- 4 tablespoons olive oil
- 1 onion, chopped
- 1 -2 teaspoon dried oregano
- 3 crushed garlic cloves
- Black pepper, to taste
- 1 cup white rice
- 2 cups chicken broth
- 1 lemon juice
- 4 ounces feta cheese
- Salt, to taste

## Directions

1. Heat olive oil over medium heat in a skillet and add onions.
2. Cook the onions and add lemon juice, salt, oregano, black pepper, and garlic.
3. Cook the ingredients until the aroma comes.
4. Next, add lemon juice, rice, and broth.
5. Let it simmer and cook for 15 minutes.
6. Once it's cooked, top with feta cheese.
7. Serve and enjoy.

# 26. Mediterranean Cauliflower Fried Rice

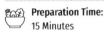 **Preparation Time:** 15 Minutes |  **Cooking Time:** 25 Minutes |  **Servings:** 4

## Ingredients

- 1 cup shredded cauliflower
- 1 cup shredded broccoli
- 1 cup carrots, shredded
- 2 teaspoons herbs de Provence
- 1/2 cup cherry tomatoes
- 1/2 cup kalamata olives
- 1/3 cup feta cheese
- 1 tablespoon parsley
- 2 teaspoons olive oil, extra virgin
- 1/4 cup chopped onion
- 1/2 tablespoon lemon juice
- Salt and pepper, to taste

## Directions

1. Heat the oil in a skillet over medium flame.
2. Add onions to it and cook for 2 minutes.
3. Next, put in the tomatoes and cook for 5 minutes.
4. Now at this stage, add shredded cauliflower, carrots, and broccoli
5. And cook until tender
6. Then add the herbs de Provence, lemon juice, olives, listed remaining seasoning, and parsley.
7. Stir well and add cooked rice.
8. Stir until all the ingredients are combined.
9. Serve it with cheese as a top.

# 27. Rice, Potato, and Fish Mix (GF and DF)

 **Preparation Time:** 35 Minutes |  **Cooking Time:** 45 Minutes |  **Servings:** 4

## Ingredients

- 1 cup rice, presoaked
- 2 cups water
- 1 cup of spinach
- 1 cup sweet potato, sliced or cubed
- 1-1/2 cup code fish, crumble
- Paprika, to taste
- Salt, to taste
- ½ cup olive oil

## Directions

1. Heat oil in a large pan and cook potatoes until brown.
2. Boil water in a pot and add spinach to it. Cook until soft for 25 minutes.
3. Then add the fish to a frying pan and add oil.
4. Crumble the fish and add it to a large rice pot.
5. Add in the rice and pour in the 2 cups of water
6. Cook rice and cod fish together for 15 minutes.
7. Now drain spinach and set it aside.
8. Add spinach, cooked sweet potatoes, and cod rice in a large skillet, and mix well.
9. Add salt and paprika.
10. Stir and serve.

# 28. Rice with Cashews and Pecans

 **Preparation Time:** 25 Minutes |  **Cooking Time:**

## Ingredients

- 2 cups raw rice, presoaked
- ½ cup cashew, sliced
- 1 cup onion
- 12 ounces of chicken broth
- 1/2 cup water
- 2 tbsp red wine
- 1 tsp thyme leaves
- 2 cups fennel
- 1 cup dried cranberries
- 1/2 cup pecans

## Directions

1. Roast the cashews and pecans in a cooking pan over medium heat.
2. Then, transfer it to a bowl.
3. Add more oil to the pan and cook the onions.
4. Once the onions get translucent, add the rice, and cook for 5 minutes.
5. Now add the chicken broth, red wine, broth, and thyme.
6. Cook the rice until the liquid evaporates.
7. Add the fennel and cranberries at this stage
8. Preheat the oven to 340 degrees F.
9. Place the mixture into the large casserole dish and bake for 45 minutes.
10. Then add the roasted cashews and pecans to the rice.
11. Serve hot.

# 29. Grilled Chicken Tzatziki Sauce with Yellow Rice

 **Preparation Time:** 25 Minutes |  **Cooking Time:** 65-70 Minutes |  **Servings:** 6

## Ingredients

- 2 teaspoons of avocado
- 1 sweet onion finely diced
- 4 cloves garlic crushed
- ¼ teaspoon of turmeric
- ¼ teaspoon of cumin
- 1/3 teaspoon paprika
- Salt, to taste
- 1 -1/2 cups basmati rice, rinsed and drained
- 2.5 cups water

- 4 teaspoons of cilantro finely chopped
- 4 teaspoons of parsley flat-leaf, finely chopped
- 1/2 cup pine nuts, toasted
- 1 pound of grilled chicken
- Ingredients for tzatziki sauce
- 1 cup cucumber, finely grated
- 1 cup Greek yogurt
- 2 tablespoons lemon juice
- ½ tablespoon olive oil, extra-virgin
- 2 garlic cloves, grated
- Pinch of sea salt
- ½ tablespoon dill, chopped
- 1 tablespoon mint, chopped

## Directions

1. Heat oil in a large cooking pan and sauté onions in it
2. Then add garlic and cook until aroma comes.
3. Add in cumin, turmeric, salt, and paprika.
4. Cook for 1 minute.
5. Then pour in the water and scrape the sides of the pan.
6. Stir and simmer the mixture,
7. Now add rice and let the water evaporate.
8. Now, cover and cook the rice for 20 minutes.
9. Meanwhile, mix all the sauce ingredients in a bowl and stir well.
10. Garnish with chopped cilantro, parsley, and pine nuts.
11. Serve immediately with Tzatziki sauce, and grilled chicken
12. Enjoy!

## CHAPTER NO 8

# 20 Seafood Recipes

## 1. Tuna with Dijon Vinaigrette (GF and DF)

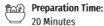 **Preparation Time:** 20 Minutes |  **Cooking Time:** 12 Minutes |  **Servings:** 2

### Ingredients

- 1 pound of salmon, cubed
- Salt and black pepper, to taste
- 2 teaspoons of olive oil
- For Mustard Dressing
- 4 teaspoons Dijon mustard
- 1 lime zest
- 2 lemon juice
- 1 cup extra virgin olive oil
- ½ teaspoons sumac
- Salt and black pepper, to taste
- For the Salad
- 2 cucumbers, peeled and cubed
- 6 radishes, peeled and cubed
- 2 green onions, chopped
- ½ red onion, peeled and chopped
- ½ cup Kalamata olives, chopped
- ½ cup parsley, chopped
- 10 mint leaves, chopped
- Side servings:
- Few Heirloom tomatoes, as needed
- Few Pita chips, as needed for servings

### Directions

1. Preheat the oven to 350 degrees F.
2. Season the salmon with salt, pepper, and olive oil.
3. Bake it in the oven for 12 minutes or more.
4. Mix the olive oil, Dijon mustard, salt, pepper, sumac, pepper, lemon zest, and lemon juice. Mix it well.
5. Take a bowl and add all the salad ingredients to it.
6. Pour the dressing over the salad and toss.
7. Serve the salmon with salad, pita chips, and heirloom tomatoes.

## 2. Mediterranean Seafood Stew (GF and DF)

 **Preparation Time:** 25 Minutes | 20-25 Minutes | **Servings:** 6 | **Cooking Time:**

## Ingredients

- 2 cups potatoes, peeled and cubed
- 2 tablespoons olive oil, or as needed
- 2 medium onions, cut in half and thinly sliced
- 4 teaspoons red pepper
- 4 cloves garlic, minced, or more to taste
- 16 ounces of tomatoes
- 1 cup dry white wine
- 1-1/2 cup fish stock
- 12 ounces white fish, cut into small chunks
- 2 pounds of clams in the shell, scrubbed
- 12 ounces shrimp, peeled and deveined
- 8 ounces calamari, sliced into thin rings
- ¼ cup parsley, chopped and fresh
- 1 lemon, juiced
- 1-1/2 teaspoons lemon zest
- Salt and ground black pepper to taste

## Directions

1. Take a large cooking pot and pour in the water along with some salt.
2. Let it boil, and add potatoes for cooking.
3. Once the potatoes get cooked, drain, and set them aside.
4. Heat olive oil in a skillet and add onions for cooking.
5. Then add garlic and cook for 5 to 7 minutes.
6. Now add the tomatoes, boiled potatoes, and white wine. Bring all this to a simmer.
7. Pour in stock and fish.
8. Simmer for 4 minutes and add clams, calamari, and shrimp.
9. Cook for 6 minutes.
10. Then remove and discard unopened clams.
11. Top with parsley, lemon juice, lemon zest, and basil.
12. Adjust the seasoning and serve.

# 3. Mediterranean Pan-Roasted Salmon (GF and DF)

| 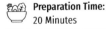 Preparation Time: 20 Minutes |  Cooking Time: 10-15 Minutes |  Servings: 4 |
|---|---|---|

## Ingredients

- 1 teaspoon basil leaves
- 1 teaspoon garlic powder
- 1/2 teaspoon oregano leaves
- 1/2 teaspoon rosemary
- 1 teaspoon sea salt
- 4 large salmon fillets
- 1 tablespoon olive oil
- 2 tablespoons sugar
- 1 tablespoon of fennel
- 2 cups cherry tomatoes
- Lemon wedges

## Directions

1. Mix the first five ingredients in a large bowl.
2. Coat the salmon with it.
3. Save some for further use.
4. Heat half the oil in a skillet and cook the fish for 5 minutes per side.
5. Next, add sugar and remaining oil along with the reserved seasoning mixture.
6. Next, add the cherry tomatoes and fennel.
7. Cook everything for 5 minutes
8. Then serve with lemon wedges.

# 4. Tuna, Egg, and Cheese (GF)

|  Preparation Time: 15 Minutes |  Cooking Time: 0 Minutes |  Servings: 1 |
|---|---|---|

## Ingredients

- 1 can of non-salted tuna, drained
- 2 boiled eggs, diced
- 2 tablespoons light mayonnaise
- 1 cup carrots, grated
- Pinch of sea salt
- Pepper to taste
- Ingredients for Garnishing
- Red chilies cut into cubes
- ½ cup feta, crumbled

## Directions

1. Cut the eggs in half.
2. Add the yolk to a bowl and mix in the remaining ingredients.
3. Fill the cavity of egg whites with this mixture.
4. Sprinkle red chilies and feta cheese.
5. Serve.

# 5. Mediterranean Style

# Shrimp Recipe (GF and DF)

 **Preparation Time:** 25 Minutes |  **Cooking Time:** 6-15 Minutes | **Servings:** 4

## Ingredients

- 2 pounds of large shrimp peeled and deveined
- Salt and black pepper to taste
- 1 teaspoon allspice
- ½ teaspoon of oregano
- 2 teaspoons of lemon juice of
- 4 tablespoon olive oil
- 1 white onion sliced
- 6 mini peppers sliced
- 4 cloves garlic minced
- ½ teaspoon of cumin
- 1 teaspoon coriander
- ½ teaspoon nutmeg
- 3 large tomatoes cut into chunks
- ½ cup water

## Directions

1. Season the shrimp with salt, allspice, pepper, lemon juice, oregano, and 1 tablespoon of olive oil.
2. Heat the remaining oil in a skillet and sauté onions in it.
3. Cook for 5 minutes.
4. Then add garlic and pepper, nutmeg, cumin, and coriander.
5. Sauté them for about 5 minutes.
6. Then put in the shrimp and the tomatoes.
7. Pour in the water and let it cook at low for 6 -10 minutes
8. Once tomatoes get soft, serve, and enjoy.
9.

# 6. Mediterranean Grouper (GF)

 **Preparation Time:** 25 Minutes |  **Cooking Time:** 20-30 Minutes |  **Servings:** 4

## Ingredients

- 2 teaspoons olive oil more for coating fish
- 2-4 garlic cloves

---

- 1/4 teaspoon dried red chili
- 1 cup cherry tomatoes
- 2-4 tablespoons capers
- 1/2 cup kalamata olives
- Salt and black pepper, to taste
- 2 teaspoons white wine
- 2 teaspoons oregano
- 2 teaspoons parsley
- Slices of Baguette
- 4 grouper fish fillets
- Ingredients for tzatziki sauce
- 1 cup cucumber, finely grated
- 1 cup Greek yogurt
- 2 tablespoons lemon juice
- ½ tablespoon olive oil, extra-virgin
- 2 garlic cloves, grated
- Pinch of sea salt
- ½ tablespoon dill, chopped
- 1 tablespoon mint, chopped

## Directions

1. Mix all the sauce ingredients in a bowl and set aside for further use.
2. Fold two parchment papers from a circle.
3. Season the fillets with some oil, salt, and black pepper.
4. Put the fillet inside the parchment paper.
5. Heat olive oil in a skillet over medium heat.
6. Sauté garlic in it
7. Then add red chilies
8. Cook for 1 minute
9. Turn off the flame and add olives, tomato, and capers.
10. Put the tomato mixture over the fish fillets
11. Pour 2 teaspoons of wine
12. And add the oregano and parsley on top.
13. Now, fold the foil and steam the fish in a steamer for 20 minutes
14. Serve with baguette slices and serves with already prepared sauce.

# 7. Grilled Swordfish Recipe with a Mediterranean Twist (GF and DF)

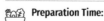 **Preparation Time:** 15 Minutes |  **Cooking Time:**

 10-15 Minutes   **Servings:** 2

## Ingredients

- 4 garlic cloves
- 1cup extra virgin olive oil
- 2 tablespoons lemon juice
- 1 teaspoon coriander
- 1 teaspoon cumin
- 1 teaspoon sweet paprika
- Salt and black pepper, to taste
- 4 swordfish steaks
- Red pepper flakes

## Directions

1. Add olive oil, garlic, oil, listed spices, salt, pepper, and lemon juice to the high-speed food processor and pulse it.
2. Brush the fish with the blended marinade.
3. Refrigerate it for 10 minutes.
4. Preheat the grill and grill the fish for 5 minutes per side.
5. Once done, serve.

## 8. Baked White Fish (GF and DF)

 **Preparation Time:** 10 Minutes  |  **Cooking Time:** 15-20 Minutes  |  **Servings:** 4

## Ingredients

- ¾ cup black olives pitted
- 1 cup sun-dried tomatoes in olive oil, drained and roughly chopped
- 2 tablespoons capers, drained
- 2 cloves of garlic
- 4 tablespoons parsley
- Salt and black pepper, to taste
- 2 tablespoons lemon juice
- 4 tablespoons olive oil
- 4 white fish filets (5 ounces each)

## Directions

1. Preheat the oven to 400 degrees F.
2. Combine capers, basil, olives, garlic, sundried tomatoes, lemon juice, and olive oil in a food processor.
3. Pulse it slightly.

4. Season the fish with olive oil, salt, and black pepper.
5. 2-3 tablespoons of the blended spread on top of each fish.
6. Let it sit in refrigerators for a few minutes.
7. Bake in the oven for 15 minutes, flipping halfway
8. Then serve with parsley.

## 9. Easy Shrimp Scampi (GF and DF)

 **Preparation Time:** 10 Minutes  |  **Cooking Time:** 8-12 Minutes  |  **Servings:** 3

## Ingredients

- 1.5-pound large shrimp, peeled and deveined
- 4 large garlic cloves, minced
- Salt and black pepper, to taste
- 2 tablespoons extra virgin olive oil
- 1 teaspoon red pepper flakes, or more to your liking
- 2 tablespoons butter, plant-based butter
- ¼ cup vegetable broth
- 1 lemon juice
- 1 lemon zest
- ½ cup fresh parsley, chopped

## Directions

1. Season the shrimp with salt, black pepper, and olive oil.
2. Toss it well and refrigerate it for 20 minutes.
3. Heat the remaining olive oil in a skillet and cook the shrimp for 2 minutes.
4. Remove and set aside for further use.
5. Now in the same skillet, add garlic and pepper flakes, and cook for 2 minutes.
6. Add olive oil and butter and cook it for 1 more minute.
7. Add the shrimp back and stir the ingredients.
8. Then serve immediately with a drizzle of lemon zest, lemon juice, and fresh parsley.

## 10. Poached Halibut Salad with Meyer Lemon Vinaigrette (GF and DF)

  **Preparation Time:** 10 Minutes  |   **Cooking Time:** 5-10 Minutes  |   **Servings:** 2

## Ingredients

- 2 halibut fillets
- 2 cups arugula
- 2 Mache lettuces
- 3 sliced radishes
- 3 cherry tomatoes
- 2 shallots
- 2 tablespoons chopped fresh dill
- Ingredients to garnish
- Parsley leaves, few
- Lemon vinaigrette Ingredients
- 2 Lemons, juice
- 2 tablespoons of Olive oil
- 1/4 teaspoons mustard
- Salt and black pepper, to taste

## Directions

1. Combine Lemon vinaigrette ingredients in a bowl and set aside.
2. Pour water into a pan and bring it to a boil.
3. Put the fish fillet into the pan and reduce the flame.
4. Let it cook for 5 minutes.
5. Now place greens in the bowl and add the remaining ingredients on top.
6. Once the fish is cooked, add it to the top.
7. Season it with salt and pepper.
8. Pour the dressing over the fish.
9. Serve the fish with greens.
10. Enjoy!

# 11. Seared Salmon with Arugula Salad (GF)

 **Preparation Time:** 15 Minutes |  **Cooking Time:** 12 Minutes |  **Servings:** 3

## Ingredients

- 3 salmon fillets
- Salt and black pepper, to taste
- 1-1/2 tablespoons oregano
- ½ tablespoon garlic powder
- ½ teaspoon paprika
- 2 teaspoons of olive oil for searing
- 2 teaspoons of Lemon juice, or as needed
- Salad ingredients
- 2 cups Arugula, washed, dried, and torn

---

- 1/3 cup extra-virgin olive oil
- 1 lemon, juiced
- Salt and black pepper, to taste
- 1/3 cup of Parmigiano-Reggiano

## Directions

1. Season the salmon with salt and black pepper.
2. Take a bowl and add garlic, paprika, and oregano and mix well.
3. Rub the mixture all over the salmon.
4. Now heat olive oil in a skillet and add salmon to it.
5. Cook the salmon from both sides.
6. Just before taking out the salmon, squeeze lemon juice on top.
7. Now mix all the salad ingredients in a bowl and serve with salmon.

# 12. Fish with Wilted Greens and Mushrooms (GF and DF)

 **Preparation Time:** 25 Minutes |  **Cooking Time:** 20 Minutes |  **Servings:** 2-4

## Ingredients

- 3 tablespoons olive oil, divided
- ½ large sweet onion, sliced
- 3 cups sliced cremini mushrooms
- 2 cloves garlic, sliced
- 4 cups chopped kale
- 1 medium tomato, diced
- 2 teaspoons Mediterranean Herb Mix
- 1 tablespoon lemon juice
- ½ teaspoon salt, divided
- ½ teaspoon ground pepper, divided
- 4 (4 ounces) cod fish fillets
- Chopped fresh parsley for garnish

## Directions

1. Heat oil in a skillet and cook onions in it for 2 minutes.
2. Add garlic and then add the mushrooms
3. Now cook it for 4 minutes
4. Then add the tomatoes, kale, tomato, and half of the herb mix.
5. Once the kale is cooked, add lemon juice, salt, and pepper

6. Season the fish with salt, black pepper, and the remaining herb mix
7. Heat the remaining oil in a skillet and cook the fish for 4 minutes per side.
8. Top the fish with the vegetables, and serve with a topping of parsley; enjoy.

# 13. Grilled Shrimp Skewers (GF and DF)

 **Preparation Time:** 10 Minutes |  **Cooking Time:** 8 Minutes |  **Servings:** 4

## Ingredients

- For The Marinade
- ½ cup extra virgin olive oil
- 2 Lemon zest
- 5 crushed garlic cloves
- 1/2 cup chopped fresh parsley
- 1 teaspoon oregano
- 1 teaspoon paprika
- 1 teaspoon coriander
- 1 teaspoon red pepper flakes
- For the Shrimp
- 3-4 cups of shrimp
- Kosher salt

## Directions

1. Preheat the grill.
2. Combine all the marinade ingredients in a bowl.
3. Marinate shrimp in it for a few hours in the refrigerator.
4. Put the shrimp on its skewers.
5. Mist the grill with oil spray.
6. Cook the shrimp on the grill for 4 minutes per side.
7. Once done, serve.

# 14. Grilled Cod with Lemon and Parsley (GF and DF)

 **Preparation Time:** 15 Minutes |  **Cooking Time:** 10 Minutes |  **Servings:** 4

## Ingredients

- 2 pounds cod fillets
- 4 tablespoons olive oil
- 1 lemon juice

- 1 teaspoon dried parsley
- 4 teaspoons of green onions
- Salt and black pepper, to taste

## Directions

1. Preheat the grill grates for a few minutes.
2. Combine the parsley, olive oil, lemon juice, and onions in a large bowl.
3. Season the cod fillet with salt and pepper.
4. Grill the cod fish for 5 minutes per side on a grill.
5. Brush the fish with olive oil and lemon mixture during the cooking process.
6. Serve and enjoy!

# 15. Black Sea Bass Recipe

 **Preparation Time:** 12 Minutes |  **Cooking Time:** 15-18 Minutes | **Servings:** 2

## Ingredients

- 4 black sea bass fillets
- 1/4 cup olive oil
- 1 cup Panko breadcrumbs
- 1/3 cup Parmesan cheese
- 1/3 teaspoons garlic powder
- 1/3 teaspoon dried parsley
- 1/3 teaspoon thyme
- 2 teaspoons sweet paprika
- Salt and black pepper, to taste

## Directions

1. Preheat the oven to 350 degrees F.
2. Combine paprika, salt, breadcrumbs, olive oil, garlic powder, cheese, thyme, parsley, and black pepper in a bowl.
3. Then brush the filet with this mixture.
4. Bake the fish in the oven for 15 -18 minutes, flipping halfway.
5. Serve it and enjoy.

# 16. Salmon with Roasted Red Pepper Quinoa Salad (DF)

 **Preparation Time:** 12 Minutes |  **Cooking Time:** 8-10 Minutes |  **Servings:** 5

## Ingredients

- 2 tablespoons extra-virgin olive oil, divided
- 1-1/2 pounds skin-on salmon, preferably wild, cut into 4 portions
- Salt and black pepper, to taste
- 4 tablespoons red-wine vinegar
- 2 cloves of garlic, grated
- 2 cups of quinoa, cooked
- 1 cup red bell peppers, chopped
- ¼ cup fresh cilantro, chopped
- ½ cup pistachios, chopped toasted

## Directions

1. Season the fish with salt and black pepper
2. Heat oil in a skillet and add salmon for cooking, 4 minutes per side.
3. Combine the remaining oil, garlic, salt, pepper, and vinegar in a medium bowl.
4. Then put in the peppers, quinoa, cilantro, and pistachios; toss well.
5. Serve it with cooked salmon.
6.

# 17. Mediterranean Halibut Sandwiches (GF and DF)

 **Preparation Time:** 20 Minutes |  **Cooking Time:** 20 Minutes |  **Servings:** 4

## Ingredients

- 2 pounds of Halibut
- Salt and black pepper to taste
- 1 loaf of bread, sliced
- 2 tablespoons of olive oil
- 4 Garlic cloves, minced
- 1 cup Mayonnaise
- 6 Sun-dried tomatoes, chopped
- 1 tablespoon Basil, fresh
- 1 teaspoon of parsley, fresh and chopped
- Few Capers, chopped
- ¼ teaspoon of Lemon zest

## Directions

1. Preheat the oven to 350 degrees F.
2. Mist the baking tray with oil spray.

3. Season the halibut with some olive oil, salt, and black pepper.
4. Add it to the baking tray and cook for 15 minutes.
5. Toast the bread in the toaster and rub it with garlic.
6. Add tomatoes, parsley, basil, lemon zest, capers, and mayonnaise to a bowl.
7. Layer the fish onto toasted bread and top with bowl mixture.
8. Enjoy.

# 18. Parmesan Shrimp (GF)

 **Preparation Time:** 15 Minutes |  **Cooking Time:** 10 Minutes |  **Servings:** 4

## Ingredients

- 1.5-pound jumbo shrimp, peeled and deveined
- Salt and black pepper
- 1 teaspoon of olive oil
- ½ teaspoon of red pepper flakes, to taste
- 4 large garlic cloves, crushed or minced
- Garlic parmesan sauce:
- 1/3 cup chopped parsley, optional
- 1 lemon, zest, and juice
- Few teaspoons of extra virgin olive oil
- 1 teaspoon oregano
- ½ cup grated parmesan, more to your liking

## Directions

1. Preheat the grill grates for a few minutes.
2. Combine the garlic parmesan sauce ingredients n a large bowl.
3. Season the shrimp with salt, olive oil, garlic, red pepper flakes, and pepper.
4. Grill the shrimp for 5 minutes per side on a grill.
5. Then toss the shrimp in the garlic parmesan sauce.
6. Serve.

# 19. Ginger Shrimp

 **Preparation Time:** 10 Minutes |  **Cooking Time:** 10 Minutes |  **Servings:** 4

## Ingredients

- 3 pounds shrimp, peeled and deveined

- 2 teaspoons fresh ginger, chopped
- Salt, to taste
- White pepper, to taste
- 1 cup water
- 2 teaspoons potato starch
- 4 teaspoons brown sugar
- 4 teaspoons olive oil
- 1 cup onion, sliced
- 4 garlic cloves, minced

## Directions

1. Combine shrimp, fresh ginger, black pepper, salt, and white pepper, and mix.
2. In a bowl, combine water, potato starch, sugar, garlic cloves, and half of the olive oil.
3. Add shrimp to the bowl mixture.
4. Now heat the remaining olive oil in a skillet and sauté the onions.
5. Cook the shrimp mixture for 5 minutes per side.
6. Serve and enjoy.

# 20. Rice Chickpeas and Fish Recipe

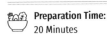 **Preparation Time:** 20 Minutes  **Cooking Time:** 35-40 Minutes  **Servings:** 4

## Ingredients

- 2 tablespoons of Extra Virgin Olive Oil
- 4 garlic cloves
- 4 tablespoons tomato paste
- 4 tomatoes
- ½ sliced red pepper
- 14-ounce chickpeas
- 2 cup water
- 1 tablespoon of Cilantro
- Salt and black pepper to taste
- 2 teaspoons Rap El Hangout
- 2 pounds of cod fillet
- ½ teaspoon paprika
- ½ teaspoon cumin
- 2 tablespoons of lemon juice
- 2 cups brown rice, cooked

## Directions

1. Heat olive oil in a cooking pan or skillet over medium heat.
2. Add garlic and cook until aroma comes.
3. Then put in the bell peppers, tomato paste, and tomatoes.
4. Cook for 7 minutes and dump in the chickpeas with water.
5. Season it with salt, cumin, paprika, and pepper.
6. Then after 2 minutes add the Raps El Hangout, and cook for 10 minutes over low heat.
7. Add the fish to the chickpea mixture and pour in the lemon juice.
8. Cook for 15 minutes
9. Once done, serve it with cilantro.
10. Serve over rice and enjoy.

# CHAPTER NO 9

# 10 Dessert Recipes

## 1. Ergolavi (GF)

 **Preparation Time:** 22 Minutes |  **Cooking Time:** 20-25 Minutes | **Servings:** 3

### Ingredients

- 6 cups almonds
- 2.5 cups sugar
- 4 small egg whites
- 1-1/4 teaspoons vanilla

### Directions

1. Preheat the oven 0 300 degrees F
2. Pulverize the almonds in a high-speed blender.
3. Now combine egg white and sugar in a bowl and whisk.
4. Then add almonds and vanilla.
5. Blend to make the dough.
6. Shape into fingers.
7. Layer it 0 to a baking sheet lined with butter paper.
8. Bake in the oven for 20-25 minutes,
9. Once it did, serve.

## 2. Berry Compote (GF)

 **Preparation Time:** 22 Minutes |  **Cooking Time:** 45 Minutes |  **Servings:** 4

### Ingredients

- 12 ounces of strawberries, hulled and cubed
- 12 ounces of blueberries
- 12 ounces of raspberries
- 4 tablespoons of coconut sugar
- 2 tablespoons of lime juice
- 4 cups of Greek yogurt

### Directions

1. Preheat the oven to 400 degrees F
2. Combine berries and sugar in a bowl and add lime juice
3. Add it to a large baking dish
4. Bake in the oven for 30 to 45 minutes
5. Check every 15 minutes
6. Once done, let it cool for about 15 to 20 minutes
7. Serve with Greek yogurt.

# 3. Honey Almond Ricotta with Fruits

 **Preparation Time:** 15 Minutes | **Cooking Time:** 0 Minutes | **Servings:** 2

## Ingredients

- For the ricotta spread
- 2 cups ricotta
- ½ cup sliced almonds
- 1/2 teaspoon almond extract
- 2 teaspoons honey
- 1 teaspoon of Orange zest
- 1 orange, juice,
- For Servings
- 2 Whole grain toasts
- Few Peaches (sliced)
- Few teaspoons of Honey (to drizzle)

## Directions

1. Combine the cheese, almonds, zest, and its orange extract in a mixing bowl
2. Mix to combine.
3. Serve it over toast with peaches and honey drizzle.
4. Serve.

# 4. Orange Cookies

 **Preparation Time:** 20 Minutes |  **Cooking Time:** 25 Minutes |  **Servings:** 4

## Ingredients

- 8 ounces butter
- 1 cup sugar
- 2 eggs, whisked
- ½ orange's zest and juice
- 1/4 teaspoon vanilla extract
- 4 tablespoon mastic liqueur (optional)
- 22 ounces of whole wheat flour
- 2 tablespoon baking powder

## Directions

1. Combine all the ingredients in a large bowl and mix well.
2. Shape into cookies.
3. Line the base of the baking tray with parchment paper,

4. Bake for around 25-28 minutes in preheated oven at 375 degrees F.
5. Serve.

# 5. Greek Yogurt Dessert

 **Preparation Time:** 25 Minutes |  **Cooking Time:** 0 Minutes |  **Servings:** 2

## Ingredients

- 1 pound strained Greek yogurt
- 26 ounces milk, condensed
- ½ Lemon zest and juice
- 16-ounce biscuits (vegan based)
- 1 cup chocolate shaving, 80 % cacao

## Directions

1. Combine the Greek yogurt, milk, and zest in a bowl.
2. Mix until it forms a creamy paste.
3. Once it turns into mousse consistency.
4. Layer the bottom with crushed biscuits in a serving bowl and add to the yogurt mixture.
5. Serve with a garnish of dark chocolate shaving.

# 6. Browned Financiers

 **Preparation Time:** 20 Minutes |  **Cooking Time:** 15 Minutes |  **Servings:** 2

## Ingredients

- 1 cup almond, powdered or almond flour
- ¾ cup sugar
- 4 tablespoons whole wheat flour
- Salt, to taste
- 4 large and organic eggs (large)
- ½ teaspoon vanilla extract
- 2 tablespoons of coconut oil
- Oil spray for greasing

## Directions

1. Preheat the oven to around 370 degrees.
2. Grease 24 mini muffin tins with oil spray.
3. Combine the sugar, almond powder, whole wheat flour, and salt.
4. In a separate bowl, whisk egg whites and vanilla extract
5. Add to it the coconut oil and combine it with the flour mixture.

6. Fill the mixture into greased muffin tins.
7. Bake it for 15 minutes
8. Take out, let it cool, and serve.

## 7. Peach Nectarine Mango Crumble (GF)

 **Preparation Time:**
30 Minutes

 **Cooking Time:**
28 Minutes

 **Servings:**
2

### Ingredients

- 1 large mango cubed
- 2 peaches, peeled cubed
- 4 nectarines, seedless and cubed
- 3 ounces brown sugar
- 3 ounces flour
- 3-ounce almond butter
- 8 cookies, vegan cookies

### Directions

1. Chop the fruits into small cubes and add them to a dish.
2. Preheat the oven to 350 degrees F.
3. Crumble the cookies and add the flour and sugar
4. Then add almond butter and mix well.
5. Top the crumble with the fruits.
6. Add it to the oven and bake it for around 28-30 minutes.
7. Once done, serve.

## 8. Lavender Honey Ice Cream (GF)

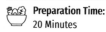 **Preparation Time:**
20 Minutes

 **Cooking Time:**
10 Minutes

 **Servings:**
4

### Ingredients

- 12 ounces of whole milk
- 2-4 ounces of yogurt
- 4 cups cream
- 2 ounces honey
- 1 teaspoon dried lavender

### Directions

1. Mix milk with honey, lavender, and cream.
2. Heat a pan until 185 degrees F
3. Add the mixture of it and keep stirring

4. Once it's cooked, remove it from the heat.
5. Then add the yogurt once it cools down.
6. Let it sit in the fridge for at least overnight.
7. The next day add it to the ice cream mixture at low speeds,
8. Again freeze it in the freezer.
9. Then serve.

## 9. Crème Brule (GF)

 **Preparation Time:**
20 Minutes

 **Cooking Time:**
50-60 Minutes

 **Servings:**
4

### Ingredients

- 8 large egg yolks
- 2 cups whipping cream
- 1 tablespoon vanilla extract
- 1/3 cup brown sugar

### Directions

1. Preheat the oven to 350 degrees F.
2. Take a bowl and beat eggs in it.
3. Now mix sugar into eggs and mix until eggs are dissolved.
4. Now put in the whipping cream and the vanilla extract.
5. Let it stir well.
6. Pass this mixture through a strainer and then shift it to a custard cup.
7. Get rid of bubbles. Do to fill till up.
8. Add these ramekins to the pan and pour hot water to cover half of the ramekins.
9. Add it to the oven and bake for 50 minutes.
10. Once done, let it cool and put it in the fridge for about 4 hours.
11. Once done, serve.

# 10. Lemon Meringue (GF)

**Preparation Time:** 5 Minutes | **Cooking Time:** 10 Minutes | **Servings:** 2

## Ingredients

- 2 egg whites
- 3-ounce castor sugar
- 2-ounce water
- 2-ounce lemon juice

## Directions

1. Pour water into a large cooking pan and add sugar.
2. Let it cook until sugar is dissolved, add lemon juice, and let it simmer for a while.
3. Meanwhile, whisk egg whites in a bowl until a stiff peak forms on top.
4. Add these to the pan and turn off the heat.
5. Now mix it up until the temperature drops to room temperature.
6. Use a torch to bake it from the top.
7. Serve.

**CHAPTER NO 10**

# 10 Snacks and Appetizer

## 1. Almond Butter, Berries, and Banana Yogurt Bowl (GF)

 **Preparation Time:** 5 Minutes |  **Cooking Time:** 0 Minutes |  **Servings:** 4

### Ingredients

- 4 cups Greek yogurt
- 2 medium bananas, peeled and sliced
- 1 cup strawberries, chopped
- ¼ cup almond butter
- ¼ cup Flax seed meal

### Directions

1. Take a serving bowl and add Greek yogurt as a base.
2. Now mix almond butter with flax seeds and add it to yogurt.
3. Mix it well; now top it off with bananas and strawberries.
4. Enjoy.

## 2. Appetizing Endive Heads (GF)

 **Preparation Time:** 10 Minutes |  **Cooking Time:** 0 Minutes | **Servings:** 2

### Ingredients

- 2 endive heads
- 1 package of herbed goat cheese
- 1 package of smoked salmon

### Directions

1. Cut the ends of the endives and pull the leaves.
2. Spread the cheese on the leaves.
3. Place small salmon pieces on top.
4. Enjoy once all the leaves are prepared.

## 3. Baked Beet Chips (GF and DF)

 **Preparation Time:** 20 Minutes |  **Cooking Time:** 25 Minutes |  **Servings:** 3

## Ingredients

- 4 beets, peeled and sliced
- 2 tablespoons of olive oil
- Salt, a few pinches
- 2 tablespoons chives, dry

## Directions

1. Cut the green parts of the beets.
2. Clean and rinse the beets and leave the skin on.
3. Use a mandolin cutter to cut the beets into chips.
4. Preheat the oven to 400 degrees F.
5. Coat the beets with olive oil.
6. Bake the beets in the oven for 20 minutes.
7. Bake the beets inside the oven till they become nice and crispy.
8. The cooking time for the beets may vary due to the variation in thickness; however, it will take around 10 to 20 minutes to cook everything.
9. Meanwhile, put the salt.
10. Then season the beets with chives and salt.
11. Toss and serve.

# 4. Avocado Summer Rolls

 **Preparation Time:** Minutes    **Cooking Time:** Minutes    **Servings:** 3

## Ingredients

- 8 rounds of Rice paper wrappers
- 2 cups of smoked sliced salmon
- 2avocados, sliced
- 1 small Cucumber, peeled and cubed
- 2 cups cooked rice
- Peanut sauce or any other preferred, as needed

## Directions

1. Put the rice paper under hot water.
2. Add the paper onto the cutting board and fill each paper with an equal amount of salmon, cucumber, rice, and avocado.
3. Wrap it up.
4. Once all wraps are ready, serve with your favorite sauce.

# 5. Banana Split (GF and DF)

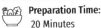 **Preparation Time:** 20 Minutes    **Cooking Time:** 10 Minutes    **Servings:** 2

## Ingredients

- 2 bananas, peeled
- 1 cup oats, cooked
- 1/3 teaspoon cinnamon
- 2 tablespoons of the almond butte

## Directions

1. Cook oats according to package instructions, and add cinnamon, bananas, and almond butter once cool down.
2. Serve.

# 6. Berries Bowl with Greek Yogurt (GF)

 **Preparation Time:** 5 Minutes    **Cooking Time:** 0 Minutes   **Servings:** 2

## Ingredients

- 1/4 cup soy milk
- 1 cup frozen blueberries
- 1 cup frozen raspberries
- 4 teaspoon porridge oats
- Toppings:
- 1 cup Greek yogurt
- 2 teaspoons of flax seeds
- 1 tablespoon of coconut flakes

## Directions

1. Add all the listed ingredients (excluding topping) to a high-speed blender and pulse until smooth.
2. Pour the mixture into a serving bowl and top with Greek yogurt, coconut flakes, and flax seeds.
3. Enjoy.

## 7. Snack Time Pumpkin Seeds (GF and DF)

 **Preparation Time:** 15 Minutes |  **Cooking Time:** 10 Minutes | **Servings:** 4

### Ingredients

- 2 cups of pumpkin seeds were rinsed and dried out
- 2 teaspoons olive oil
- Salt and black pepper to taste

### Directions

1. Combine pumpkin seeds, olive oil, salt, and pepper in a bowl.
2. Toss well and bake in the oven at 370 degrees F for 10 minutes.
3. Once it's crispy, serve.

## 8. Smoked Salmon, Avocado, and Cucumber Bites (GF and DF)

 **Preparation Time:** 20 Minutes |  **Cooking Time:** 0 Minutes |  **Servings:** 2

### Ingredients

- 1 cucumber
- 1 large avocado (peeled, pitted)
- 1 tablespoon lime juice
- 6 ounces smoked salmon, chopped
- Chives, chopped and as needed
- Salt and black pepper to taste

### Directions

1. Slice the cucumber round and ¼ inch thick cut.
2. Layer it on one large flat tray.
3. Mash avocado with lime juice and add in salmon bits.
4. Put a bite full of it over cucumber slices.
5. Garnish it with chives and season with salt and cracked black pepper.

## 9. Pumpkin Pecan Bread Pudding

 **Preparation Time:** 15 Minutes |  **Cooking Time:** 4 Hours 10 Minutes |  **Servings:** 4

### Ingredients

- 8 cups bread cubes
- ¼ cup pecans (toasted, chopped)
- 6 eggs
- 1 cup half n half
- 1 cup canned pumpkin
- 1/3 cup brown sugar
- ½ cup cacao butter
- ½ teaspoon vanilla
- ½ teaspoon cinnamon
- ½ teaspoon nutmeg
- ¼ teaspoon ginger, grounded
- 1/8 teaspoon cloves, grounded

### Directions

1. Fill the bottom of the oil grease crock pot with oil spray.
2. Cut the bread in cubed, about revealing 8 cups.
3. Whisk eggs in a bowl and add pecans, brown sugar, pumpkin, half n half, melted cacao butter, vanilla, cinnamon, nutmeg, ginger, and cloves.
4. Pour this all over bread cubes.
5. Cook at low 6 or high 4 hours.
6. Serve it with vegan ice cream and caramel.

## 10. Falafel Smash

 **Preparation Time:** 15 Minutes |  **Cooking Time:** 0 Minutes |  **Servings:** 4

### Ingredients

- 2 cups cooked chickpeas, drained
- Salt, to taste
- 1 teaspoon cumin powder
- 1 teaspoon coriander powder
- ½ teaspoon crushed red pepper
- 1 tablespoon of lemon juice
- 2 tablespoons olive oil
- ¼ cup Greek yogurt
- 1 cup of arugula

- Few pickled onions, sliced
- 4 to 6 pita bread
- For cilantro sauce:
- 2 garlic cloves, crushed
- 2 large cilantro (chopped finely, with steam)
- ¼ cup olive oil
- 2 tablespoon sesame seeds (toasted)
- Salt, pinch

## Directions

1. Mix all the cilantro sauce ingredients in a bowl and set aside for further use.

2. Mash the chickpeas in a bowl and add to the food processor
3. Add salt, cumin, and red pepper.
4. Then add lemon juice and olive oil.
5. Pulse it until smooth.
6. Spread yogurt over bread slice and layer with arugula and chickpea mixture.
7. Serve with a topping of pickled onions and cilantro sauce.

## CHAPTER NO 11

# 20 Salad Recipes

## 1. Super Avocado Salad (GF and DF)

 **Preparation Time:** 15 Minutes  **Cooking Time:** 0 Minutes  **Servings:** 4

### Ingredients

- 2 cups pre-cooked quinoa
- 2 cans of black beans
- ½ cup grape tomatoes
- 2 avocados
- ½ cup cilantro leaves
- Vinaigrette salad ingredients
- 1/4 cup lime juice
- 6 tablespoons extra-virgin olive oil
- ¼ teaspoons lime zest
- 2 garlic cloves, mooned
- Salt and black pepper to taste

### Directions

1. Combine all the salad ingredients in a large bowl.
2. In a separate small bowl, whisk vinaigrette ingredients.
3. Pour it over the salad.

4. Toss and enjoy.

## 2. Greek Kale Salad with Quinoa

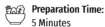 **Preparation Time:** 5 Minutes  **Cooking Time:** 0minutes  **Servings:** 3

### Ingredients

- 2 cups chopped kale
- 2 cups cooked chicken
- 2 cups cooked quinoa
- 1/4 cup red peppers
- 1/3 cup Greek salad dressing
- 1 cup feta cheese

### Directions

1. Add all listed ingredients to a large bowl and toss well.
2. Serve.

## 3. Lentil and Greens Salad with Feta and Pear (GF)

 **Preparation Time:** 15 Minutes |  **Cooking Time:** 0 Minutes |  **Servings:** 2

## Ingredients

- ½ cup lentils, cooked
- 3 cups spinach
- 4 sliced pears, chopped, peeled
- Handful of walnuts
- For the Dressing
- 4 teaspoons maple syrup
- 2 teaspoons mustard
- 2 tablespoons balsamic vinegar
- ¼ cup olive oil
- Salt and black pepper to taste

## Directions

1. Whisk all the ingredients for the dressing in a bowl
2. In another bowl, add the lentils and all the salad ingredients.
3. Drizzle the dressing over the top.
4. Enjoy.

## 4. Greek Salad with Edamame (GF and DF)

 **Preparation Time:** 5 Minutes |  **Cooking Time:** 0 Minutes |  **Servings:** 2

## Ingredients

- 1/3 cup red wine vinegar
- 4 tablespoons extra-virgin olive oil
- Salt and black pepper to taste
- 6 cups chopped romaine lettuce
- 8ounces frozen shelled edamame
- 1 cup grape tomatoes
- ½ cucumber, sliced
- 1 cup feta cheese, crumbled
- ¼ cup sliced Kalamata olives
- ¼ cup slivered red onion

## Directions

5. Combine oil, salt, pepper, and vinegar.
6. Add edamame, tomato, romaine lettuce, cucumber, feta, onions, and olives to a large bowl.
7. Mix well, and then serve.

## 5. Fig and Goat Cheese Salad (GF)

 **Preparation Time:** 5 Minutes |  **Cooking Time:** 0 Minutes |  **Servings:** 2

## Ingredients

- 4 cups mixed salad greens
- 8 dried figs, stemmed and sliced
- 2 ounces fresh goat cheese, crumbled
- 4 tablespoons of slivered almonds, preferably toasted

### Dressing Ingredients

- 4 teaspoons olive oil
- 4 teaspoons of balsamic vinegar
- 2 teaspoons honey
- Salt and black pepper to taste

## Directions

1. Mix salad greens, figs, cheese, and almonds in a bowl and toss.
2. In a separate bowl, whisk all the ingredients to drizzle.
3. Pour it over the salad and toss.
4. Serve.

## 6. White-Bean Salad with Basil Vinaigrette (GF)

 **Preparation time:** 5 minutes |  **Cooking time:** 0 minutes |  **Servings:** 2

## Ingredients

- Dressing ingredients
- 1 cup basil leaves, packed fresh
- ½ cup olive oil, extra-virgin
- 6 tablespoons red-wine vinegar
- 2 tablespoons shallot, chopped
- 4 teaspoons Dijon mustard
- 4 teaspoons honey
- Salt and pepper to taste
- Other ingredients

- 8cups mixed salad greens
- 12 ounces of cannellini beans, rinsed
- 2 cups halved cherry or grape tomatoes
- 2 cucumbers, halved lengthwise and sliced (1 cup)

## Directions

1. Take a high-speed food processor and pulse the dressing ingredients.
2. In a large bowl, add the remaining ingredients and drizzle the dressing over the top.

# 7. Easy Mediterranean Salad (GF and DF)

 **Preparation Time:** 5 Minutes     **Cooking Time:** 0 Minutes     **Servings:** 2

## Ingredients

- 8 Roma tomatoes, diced (about 3 cups diced tomatoes)
- 2 Large cucumbers, or hot-house cucumber, diced
- ½ cup chopped fresh parsley leaves
- Salt and black pepper to taste
- 1 teaspoon ground Sumac
- 4 tablespoon extra virgin olive oil
- 4 teaspoons freshly squeezed lemon juice

## Directions

1. Add the cucumber, diced tomatoes, and parsley to a large bowl.
2. Add salt and black pepper.
3. Then add olive oil, the sumac, and lemon juice.
4. Toss and serve.

# 8. Cucumber Salad (GF)

 **Preparation Time:** 5 Minutes     **Cooking Time:** 0 Minutes     **Servings:** 2

## Ingredients

- 1/3cup extra-virgin olive oil
- 4 tablespoons red-wine vinegar
- 2 tablespoon oregano, plus more for garnish
- 1 large cucumber
- Salt and black pepper to taste
- 1 cup cherry tomatoes, halved
- 1 cup red onion, sliced

---

- 1 cup feta cheese, cubed
- 1 cup pitted Kalamata olives, sliced

## Directions

1. Combine oil, salt, oregano, vinegar, and pepper in a bowl.
2. Spiral cut the cucumber lengthwise.
3. Add it to a bowl, and then add oil, vinegar sauce, tomatoes, onion, olive, and cheese.
4. Toss and serve.

# 9. Chicken Salad Recipe (GF and DF)

 **Preparation Time:** 5 Minutes     **Cooking Time:** 0 Minutes    **Servings:** 2

## Ingredients

- 2 chicken breasts, cooked and diced
- 2 apples, cored and diced
- ½ cup of celery, chopped

### Dressing Ingredients

- ½ cup of walnuts, chopped
- 4 teaspoons of lime juice
- 4 tablespoons of raw honey
- Salt and black pepper to taste
- 4 tablespoons of olive oil, extra virgin

## Directions

1. Whisk all the dressing ingredients in a bowl.
2. Add chicken breast pieces, apples, and celery to another bowl.
3. Drizzle the dressing over the top and enjoy.

# 10. Basil Spinach (GF and DF)

 **Preparation Time:** 5 Minutes     **Cooking Time:** 0 Minutes     **Servings:** 2

## Ingredients

- ½ yellow onion, diced
- 2 medium tomatoes, diced
- Handfuls of spinach washed and thawed

### Dressing Ingredients

- 1 tablespoon sesame seeds
- 2 tablespoons of olive oil

- 1/3 cup of fresh basil, finely chopped
- Salt and black pepper to taste
- Pinch of red chilies

## Directions

1. Take a bowl and add spinach, onions, and tomatoes.
2. Whisk the dressing ingredients in another bowl.
3. Drizzle the dressing over the salad bowl.
4. Serve and enjoy.

# 11. Kale Salad (GF and DF)

 **Preparation Time:** 8 Minutes    **Cooking Time:** 0 Minutes    **Servings:** 2

## Ingredients

- 2 tablespoon red onion, finely chopped
- 4 orange, peeled, seedless, and sliced
- 2 cups of kale

### Dressing Ingredients

- 2 tablespoons of olive oil
- Pinch of sea salt
- 2 lime, juiced
- ½ teaspoon of balsamic vinegar

## Directions

1. Chop the kale and add to a large bowl.
2. Then add red onions and oranges.
3. Now in a small bowl, whisk all the dressing ingredients.
4. Drizzle it over the salad.
5. Toss and enjoy.

# 12. Sunflower Sprout Salad (GF and DF)

 **Preparation Time:** 5 Minutes    **Cooking Time:** 0 Minutes    **Servings:** 4

## Ingredients

- 4 cups salad greens
- 2 cups sunflower sprouts
- 2 cups of sugar plum tomatoes, sliced in half

**Dressing ingredients**

- 4 tablespoons of
- 4 teaspoons of Olive oil
- 4 teaspoons of lemon juice, fresh and squeezed

## Directions

1. Combine mixed greens, sunflower sprouts, and plum tomatoes in a large bowl.
2. Whisk lemon juice and olive oil in a small bowl.
3. Drizzle it over the salad and toss.
4. Enjoy.

# 13. Chicken and Veggies Salad (GF)

 **Preparation Time:** 5 Minutes    **Cooking Time:** 0 Minutes    **Servings:** 4

## Ingredients

- Salad ingredients
- 2 cups of chicken, diced cooked
- 1 cup of red bell pepper, diced
- ½ artichoke heart, cooked and chopped
- 2 scallions, sliced thin, including the crisp part of the green shoot

### Dressings Ingredients

- 4 tablespoons of fresh parsley, minced
- ½ cup Lemon-Balsamic Mayonnaise, to taste
- Salt and black pepper to taste

## Directions

1. Whisk all the dressing ingredients in a bowl and set aside.
2. Mix all the salad ingredients in a large bowl, and toss the dressing over the top.
3. Mix and serve.

## 14. Vegetable Salads (GF)

 **Preparation Time:** 5 Minutes | **Cooking Time:** 0 Minutes | **Servings:** 2

### Ingredients

- Salad ingredients
- 4 cucumbers, peeled and sliced
- 4 red tomatoes, thinly sliced
- 2 cups of black olives, cut in half
- ½ red onion, thinly sliced
- 1 cup cottage cheese, broken into small pieces
- Dressing ingredients
- Salt and black pepper
- 2 lemon juices
- 2 cups Greek yogurt

### Directions

1. Combine salad ingredients in a large bowl.
2. In a separate bowl, mix all the dressing ingredients.
3. Mix the dressing with salad and enjoy

## 15. Cabbage and Orange Salad (GF and DF)

 **Preparation Time:** 5 Minutes |  **Cooking Time:** 0 Minutes |  **Servings:** 3

### Ingredients

- ½ head purple cabbage, thinly sliced
- 2 orange, peeled and sliced into segments

### Dressing Ingredients

- 4 tablespoons of olive oil
- 2 tablespoons of apple cider vinegar
- 4 tablespoons of lemon juice
- Dash of red chili powder

### Directions

1. Combine purple cabbage and oranges in a bowl and set aside.
2. Add olive oil, apple cider, lemon juice, and chili powder to a large bowl.
3. Drizzle the dressing over the cabbage and oranges.
4. Enjoy.

## 16. Mango and Cucumber Salad (GF)

 **Preparation Time:** 5 Minutes |  **Cooking Time:** 0 Minutes |  **Servings:** 2

### Ingredients

- 2 cucumbers, peeled and sliced
- 2 mango, peeled and cubed
- 1 cup strawberries

### Dressing Ingredients

- 2 tablespoons of honey
- 1 tablespoon of plum vinegar
- Salt and black Pepper, just a pinch

### Directions

1. Add the mango, strawberries, and cucumber to a bowl and toss the dressing in a separate bowl.
2. Drizzle the dressing over mango and cucumbers.
3. Serve and enjoy.

## 17. Fresh Fruit Salad (GF and DF)

 **Preparation Time:** 5 Minutes |  **Cooking Time:** 0 Minutes |  **Servings:** 4

### Ingredients

- 2 cups diced fresh pineapple
- 1-1/4 pound strawberries, hulled and sliced
- 1 cup blackberries, halved
- 2 ripe kiwis, peeled, halved, and sliced

### Directions

1. Add all the listed ingredients to a bowl and toss well.
2. Then serve fresh.

## 18. Beet, Pomegranate, and Carrot Salad (GF and DF)

 **Preparation Time:** 5 Minutes |  **Cooking Time:** 0 Minutes |  **Servings:** 6

### Ingredients

- Salad ingredients
- 4 beets, cooked, peeled, and thinly sliced
- 2 medium carrots, peeled
- 1 cup pomegranate seeds

### Dressing Ingredients

- 1 1/2 tablespoons red wine vinegar
- 2 tablespoon honey
- ½ cup extra virgin olive oil
- 1 tablespoon fresh flat-leaf parsley, chopped
- Salt and black pepper to taste
- Directions
- Combine salad ingredients in a large bowl.
- Then combine the dressing in a separate bowl.
- Toss the dressing over the salad
- Toss and serve.

# 19. Mediterranean Greek Salad (GF and DF)

 **Preparation Time:** 5 Minutes |  **Cooking Time:** 0 Minutes |  **Servings:** 2

## Ingredients

- 2 cucumbers, seeded and sliced
- 2 cups crumbled feta cheese
- 1 cup black olives, pitted and sliced
- 2 cups diced Roma tomatoes
- 1 cup diced oil-packed sun-dried tomatoes, drained, oil reserved
- ½ red onion, sliced

## Directions

1. Combine all the listed ingredients in a large bowl.
2. Toss and serve.

# 20. Shrimps with Mangos Salad (GF and DF)

 **Preparation Time:** 5 Minutes |  **Cooking Time:** 0 Minutes |  **Servings:** 4

## Ingredients

- Salad ingredients
- 2 mangos, peeled, pitted, and diced
- 2 avocados, pitted, peeled, diced
- 1 cup green onion, chopped
- 1 cup cilantro, chopped

### Dressing

- 2 tablespoons of fresh lime juice
- 4 tablespoons of olive oil
- Salt and black pepper, to taste

## Directions

1. Whisk the dressing together in a bowl.
2. Toss all the salad ingredients in a large bowl.
3. Drizzle the dressing over the top.
4. Enjoy.

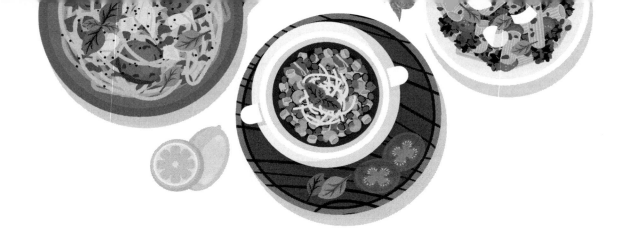

# CHAPTER NO 12

# 20 Poultry Recipes

## 1. Greek Chicken Kabobs (GF and DF)

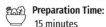 **Preparation Time:** 15 minutes |  **Cooking Time:** 10 minutes |  **Servings:** 2

### Ingredients

- For The Greek Marinade
- ½ cup red wine vinegar
- 1/2 cup olive oil
- 2 tablespoon dried oregano
- 3 garlic cloves
- 2 tablespoons finely chopped parsley
- ½ teaspoon salt
- ½ teaspoon pepper
- For The Chicken Kabobs:
- 2 pounds chopped chicken breasts
- 2 sweet chopped bell peppers
- 1 chopped onion
- 8 ounces chopped white button mushrooms

### Directions

1. Combine the Greek marinade ingredients in a bowl and set aside.
2. Arrange the chicken kabob ingredients onto skewers.
3. Preheat the grill grate and mist with oil spray.
4. Mist the skewers with oil spray.
5. Add it to the grill and cook for 5 minutes per side.
6. Baste the skewers with marinade after every 3 minutes.
7. Once done, serve and enjoy.

## 2. Baked Chicken Breast (GF and DF)

 **Preparation Time:** 15 minutes |  **Cooking Time:** 20 minutes |  **Servings:** 2-4

### Ingredients

- 4 chicken breasts
- Salt and pepper, to taste
- 3 teaspoons dry oregano
- 2 teaspoons fresh thyme
- 2 teaspoons sweet paprika
- 4 garlic cloves

- 4 tablespoons extra virgin olive oil
- 1 lemon juice
- 2 small red onions
- 8 Campari tomatoes
- Handful of Parsley
- A hand full of basil leaves

## Directions

1. Preheat the oven to 450 degrees F.
2. Use a meat mallet to flatten the chicken breasts.
3. Season it with salt and black pepper.
4. Then add salt and pepper to the chicken.
5. Combine lemon juice, spices, garlic cloves, and olive oil in the bowl.
6. Marinate the chicken in the spices mixture.
7. Put the chicken, onions, and tomatoes onto an oil-greased baking pan.
8. Bake it for 20 minutes.
9. Once done, serve with a topping of parsley and basil leaves.

# 3. Turkey Mediterranean Casserole on a Plate

 **Preparation Time:** 15 minutes  **Cooking Time:** 22-35 Minutes  **Servings:** 4

## Ingredients

- 2 pounds pasta
- 4 cups turkey meat, cooked
- 1/2 cup sun-dried tomatoes
- 12-ounce artichokes
- 16 ounces Kalamata olives
- 1 tablespoon Parsley
- 2 tablespoons fresh basil
- Salt and black pepper, to taste
- 2 cups marinara sauce
- 4 cups mozzarella cheese

## Directions

1. Preheat the oven to 370 degrees F.
2. Cook the pasta according to the package directions.
3. Add the olives, sundried tomatoes, artichokes, salt, turkey, basil, parsley, sauce, and pepper into a bowl.
4. Put the cooked and drained pasta in the casserole dish and add bowl ingredients.
5. Add cheese on top

6. Bake for 22 minutes.
7. Once done, serve and enjoy!

# 4. Mediterranean Turkey Sandwich (GF)

 **Preparation Time:** 15 Minutes  **Cooking Time:** 0 Minutes  **Servings:** 2

## Ingredients

- 2 pita buns
- ½ cup olive tapenade
- 1 cup spinach leaves
- 1 cup cucumbers
- 2 tomatoes
- 1 small onion red onions
- 1 avocado, sliced
- 2 pounds cooked turkey
- 1 cup feta cheese
- Salt and pepper, to taste

## Directions

1. Spread olive tapenade onto pita bread.
2. Add veggies and season it with salt and pepper.
3. End with the topping of turkey meat and feta cheese.
4. Serve the sandwich and enjoy!

# 5. One-Pot Chicken Pesto Pasta with Asparagus

 **Preparation Time:** 15 Minutes  **Cooking Time:** 15 Minutes  **Servings:** 2

## Ingredients

- 10 ounces penne pasta
- 1 pound asparagus
- 4 cups cooked chicken
- 1 container basil pesto
- Salt and black pepper, to taste
- 1 cup Parmesan cheese
- Basil leaves

## Directions

1. Cook the pasta according to the package directions.
2. Put the asparagus into a skillet and cook for 2 minutes in olive oil.

3. Save some pasta water once the pasta is drained.
4. Add pasta to a skillet and add chicken, salt, pepper, and pesto.
5. Now, add reserved pasta water as well.
6. Stir for 5 minutes, then add cheese and basil.
7. Serve and enjoy!

# 6. Mediterranean Chicken & Chickpea Soup (GF and DF)

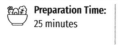 **Preparation Time:** 25 minutes    **Cooking Time:** 6 hours 10 minutes    **Servings:** 4

## Ingredients

- 4 cups chickpeas
- 4 cups water
- 2 small onions
- 2 diced tomatoes
- 4 tablespoons tomato paste
- 4 garlic cloves
- 1 bay leaf
- 2 teaspoons ground cumin
- 2 teaspoons paprika
- Salt and black pepper, to taste
- 2 pounds of chicken thighs, boneless
- 1 can artichoke hearts
- 1 cup olives
- 1/2 cup parsley

## Directions

1. Add presoaked chickpeas to a slow cooker and cook with all the listed ingredients, excluding olives, parsley, and artichokes.
2. Cook on low for 6 hours, and then release the steam naturally.
3. Then serve the stew by shredding the chicken.
4. Serve with topping parsley, olives, and artichokes.

# 7. Sicilian Olive Chicken (GF and DF)

 **Preparation Time:** 15 minutes   8 minutes   **Servings:** 4   **Cooking Time:**

## Ingredients

- 4 cups petite tomatoes soaked in Italian seasoning
- 2 cups thawed spinach
- ⅓ cup Green olives
- 1 tablespoon capers
- ¼ teaspoon red pepper
- 8 chicken cutlets
- Salt and black pepper, to taste
- 1 tablespoon extra-virgin olive oil

## Directions

1. Combine the crushed peppers, salt, pepper, tomatoes, spinach, olives, and capers in the bowl.
2. Heat the olive oil in a skillet.
3. Cook chicken in the oil for 8 minutes, then adds the bowl ingredients.
4. Cook for 5 more minutes, and then serve.

# 8. Shakshuka Recipe

 **Preparation Time:** 10 minutes    **Cooking Time:** 16 minutes    **Servings:** 4

## Ingredients

- 4 tablespoons of extra virgin olive oil
- 2 small onions, chopped
- 2 green peppers
- 4 garlic cloves
- 2 teaspoons coriander powder
- ½ teaspoon sweet paprika
- ½ teaspoons ground cumin
- Salt and black pepper
- 8 chopped tomatoes
- 1 cup tomato sauce
- 6 eggs
- ½ cup parsley leaves
- ½ cup mint leaves

## Directions

1. Heat olive oil in a skillet and add garlic to it.
2. Then sauté garlic, add green pepper, and season it with paprika, coriander, cumin, salt, and pepper.
3. Now add tomato sauce and chopped tomatoes.
4. Make holes in the skillet.
5. Now add the eggs into the holes.
6. Lower the heat and cook for 10 minutes.
7. Serve with mint and parsley.
8. Enjoy.

# 9. Mediterranean Chicken with Brussels sprouts

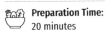 **Preparation Time:** 20 minutes |  **Cooking Time:** 35-45 minutes |  **Servings:** 2

## Ingredients

- 4 tablespoons olive oil, extra-virgin
- 2 tablespoons oregano, chopped
- 4 garlic cloves
- Salt and black pepper, to taste
- 1.5 pound Brussels sprouts
- 1 cup of gnocchi
- 1 cup sliced red onion
- 6 chicken thighs
- 1 cup cherry tomatoes
- 1 tablespoon red wine vinegar

## Directions

1. Preheat the oven to 420 degrees F.
2. Combine garlic, half of the oil, salt, pepper, Brussels sprouts, onion, oregano, and gnocchi in a large bowl and mix well.
3. Transfer it to an oil-greased baking tray.
4. Add chicken on top.
5. Cook in the oven for 15 minutes.
6. Then put in the tomatoes and onions.
7. Drizzle with oil and vinegar.
8. Cook for 20 minutes more.
9. Serve.

# 10. Chicken with Orzo Salad (GF)

 **Preparation Time:** 30 minutes |  **Cooking Time:** 45-55 minutes |  **Servings:** 4

## Ingredients

- 4 chicken breasts
- 4 tablespoons extra-virgin olive oil
- ½ teaspoon lemon zest
- Salt and black pepper
- 1.5 cups orzo
- 2 cups spinach
- 2 cups cucumber
- 2 cups tomato
- ½ cup red onion
- ½ cup crumbled feta cheese
- 6 tablespoons Kalamata olives

### Dressing Ingredients

- 4 tablespoons of olive oil
- 4 tablespoons Lemon juice
- 4 garlic cloves
- 4 tablespoons chopped fresh oregano
- Salt and black pepper, to taste

## Directions

1. Preheat the oven to 450 degrees F.
2. Season the chicken with salt, black pepper, olive oil, lemon zest, and lemon juice.
3. Mix well.
4. Then bake the chicken in the oven for 30 minutes.
5. Pour water into a pan and boil the water.
6. Cook orzo for 10 minutes, then drain and set aside,
7. Add in the spinach and cook for 1 minute.
8. Now put in the listed veggies, cheese, and olives to orzo and mix.
9. Whisk all the dressing ingredients in a bowl and pour it over the orzo salad.
10. Serve the chicken with the orzo salad.

# 11. Baked Mustard and Balsamic Chicken (GF and DF)

 **Preparation Time:**
25 Minutes

 **Cook Time:**
55 Minutes

**Servings:**
6

## Ingredients

- 2 pounds chicken thighs, boneless
- 4 tablespoons Dijon mustard
- 1/2 cup of balsamic vinegar
- ½ cup olive oil or vegetable oil
- ½ teaspoon of lemon zest
- 4 tablespoons of fresh lemon juice
- 1 tablespoon of fresh rosemary
- 4 garlic cloves, minced
- Salt and black pepper, to taste

## Directions

1. Preheat the oven to 450 degrees F.
2. In a bowl, combine olive oil, rosemary, lemon juice, zest of lemon, mustard, garlic, vinegar, salt, and black pepper, and marinate the chicken.
3. Next, mist the baking dish with olive oil and transfers the chicken to the baking dish.
4. Bake it in the oven for 50 minutes at 370 degrees F.
5. Once done, serve, and enjoy.

# 12. Creamy Chicken Soup (GF and DF)

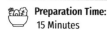 **Preparation Time:**
15 Minutes

 **Cook Time:**
25 Minutes

 **Servings:**
3

## Ingredients

- 6 cups chicken broth
- 1 pound chicken breast, shredded, boneless
- 2 green chilies, chopped and drained
- ½ cup of cauliflower florets
- ½ cup onion, diced
- 4 cloves garlic, minced
- Salt and black pepper, to taste
- 4 tablespoons of olive oil
- 1 cup coconut cream, side servings

## Directions

1. Sauté the onions in olive oil in a large cooking pot.
2. Then add garlic and cook until aroma comes.
3. Add in chicken and green chilies.
4. Let it cook for 5 minutes.
5. Then add cauliflower and broth.
6. Let the boil come.
7. Add salt and black pepper, lower the heat, and cover the pot with a lid.
8. Cook for 20 minutes.
9. Blend the soup in after taking out the chicken breast pieces.
10. Shred the pieces and transfer them back to the soup.
11. Serve it warm.

# 13. Ginger Chicken (GF and DF)

 **Preparation Time:**
20 Minutes

 **Cook Time:**
35 Minutes

 **Servings:**
3

## Ingredients

- 1.5 pounds of chicken wings, disjointed and with tips
- ½ cup of coconut amino
- 2 tablespoons maple syrup
- 2 tablespoons ginger root, minced
- 2 cloves garlic, minced
- Oil spray for greasing
- 1 tablespoon of Italian seasoning

## Directions

1. Mix maple syrup, ginger root, Italian seasoning, coconut amino, and garlic in a bowl.
2. Coat the chicken, and marinate it for 2 hours in the refrigerator.
3. Grease a baking tray with oil spray, and add chicken to it.
4. Bake it in the oven for 35 minutes at 350 degrees F.
5. Remember to flip the chicken halfway.
6. Once it's done, serve.

# 14. Coconut Creamy Chicken Cheese (GF)

 **Preparation Time:** 10 Minutes | **Cook Time:** 15 Minutes | **Servings:** 2

## Ingredients

- 2 pounds of chicken thighs, boneless
- 4 tablespoons olive oil
- 1cup coconut milk
- ½ cup chicken broth
- 2 teaspoons garlic, minced
- 4 teaspoons Italian seasoning
- ½ cup grated Parmesan cheese
- ½ cup spinach, chopped
- ½ cup cherry tomatoes halved

## Directions

1. Heat the olive oil in a skillet and cook garlic until the aroma comes.
2. Add the chicken thighs and cook until golden.
3. Pour in the chicken broth and let it cook with cover until the tenders are cooked.
4. Pour in the coconut milk and remaining ingredients, except for the Parmesan cheese.
5. Stir a few times and let the ingredients incorporate.
6. At the end, top with parmesan cheese.
7. Serve and enjoy hot.

# 15. Crispy Chicken (GF)

 **Preparation Time:** 12 Minutes  **Cook Time:** 15 Minutes  **Servings:** 4

## Ingredients

- 1.5 pounds of s chicken thigh
- 2 eggs, whisked
- ½ teaspoon oregano
- Salt and black pepper, to taste
- ½ cup almond flour
- ½ cup grated coconut
- ½ cup olive oil to fry

## Directions

1. Whisk eggs in a bowl and season it with salt, pepper, oregano
2. Add flour and coconut to a large separate bowl.

3. Dump the chicken into the egg mixture, then dredge in the flour mixture.
4. Heat olive oil in a frying pan.
5. Fry the chicken in the frying pan until brown.
6. Serve warm.

# 16. Spicy and Chunky Chicken Breast (GF)

 **Preparation Time:** 20 Minutes  **Cook Time:** 25 Minutes  **Servings:** 3

## Ingredients

- Oil spray for greasing
- For Marinating the Chicken
- 2 pounds of chicken breasts, chopped into bite-size pieces
- ½ cup fat-free Greek yogurt
- ½ tablespoon Italian seasoning
- 2 tablespoon lemon juice
- Salt and black pepper, to taste
- 1 teaspoon ground ginger
- To Make the Sauce
- 4 cloves garlic, minced
- 1/2 teaspoon paprika
- 1/6 teaspoon salt
- 2 cups coconut cream
- 1-1/4 cup parmesan cheese

## Directions

1. Combine all the chicken marinade ingredients in a large bowl and let the chicken marinade for 2 hours in the refrigerator.
2. Mix all the sauce ingredients in a separate bowl.
3. Add the marinated chicken to the baking pan grease with oil spray.
4. Bake it in the oven for 25 minutes at 375 degrees F until the internal temperature reaches 165 degrees F.
5. Serve the chicken with premade sauce.

# 17. Chicken with Avocado Pesto (GF and DF)

 **Preparation Time:** 25 Minutes  **Cook Time:** 20 Minutes  **Servings:** 2

## Ingredients

- 4 tablespoons of olive oil
- 1 teaspoon of lemon zest
- 1 teaspoon of lemon juice
- 1 pound of chicken breasts, skinless
- Salt, to taste
- Black pepper, to taste
- ¼ cup pine nuts
- 1 cup of basil leaves, fresh
- 1 cup parsley leaves, fresh
- 2 garlic cloves, minced
- 1 ripe avocado, pitted

## Directions

1. Preheat the grill to medium temperature.
2. Combine half of the lemon zest, salt, black pepper, and half of the olive oil over the chicken pieces.
3. Arrange the chicken pieces onto the bamboo skewers.
4. Pulse the parsley, pine nuts, basil, salt, pepper, lemon juices, avocado, olive oil, and garlic cloves in a blender to make a pesto sauce.
5. Grill the chicken for 7 minutes per side.
6. Once it's cooked, serve the chicken with pesto.
7. Enjoy.

# 18. Chicken Cheese Balls (GF)

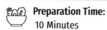 **Preparation Time:** 10 Minutes  **Cook Time:** 15 Minutes  **Servings:** 2

## Ingredients

- 1.5 pounds of chicken breast, pieces
- 1/2 cup grated cheddar cheese
- 4 eggs
- 4 tablespoons almond flour
- Salt and black pepper, to taste
- 1 cup coconut, grated
- ½ cup extra virgin olive oil to

## Directions

1. Add chicken to a food processor.
2. Then add the almond flour, coconut, cheddar cheese, salt, and black pepper.
3. Mix it all well with your hands.
4. Whisk eggs in a separate bowl.
5. Shape chicken mixture into round balls.
6. Dip the chicken balls in egg and then coat it with flour mixture.
7. Preheat a frying pan and pour olive oil into it.

8. Fry the balls until golden.
9. Serve hot.

# 19. Juicy Roasted Chicken (GF and DF)

 **Preparation Time:** 10 Minutes  **Cook Time:** 15 Minutes  **Servings:** 4

## Ingredients

- 2.5 Whole chicken, giblets removed
- Salt and black pepper to taste
- 4 tablespoons onion powder, or to taste
- ½ cup olive oil, divided
- 1 stalk of celery leaves removed

## Directions

1. Preheat the oven to 350 degrees F.
2. Season the chicken with salt, peep, onion powder, and olive oil.
3. Place the celery into the chicken cavity.
4. Bake in the oven and uncover for 1 hour until juices run clean.
5. The internal reading should be 180 degrees F
6. Allow chicken to rest for 30 minutes before serving.

# 20. Mediterranean Chicken (GF and DF)

 **Preparation Time:** 10 Minutes  **Cook Time:** 30 Minutes  **Servings:** 2

## Ingredients

- 2 tablespoons white wine
- 2 teaspoons olive oil
- 4 skinless, boneless chicken breast halves
- 2 cloves garlic, minced
- 1/4 cup diced onion
- 1.5 cups tomatoes, chopped
- ½ cup white wine
- 2 teaspoons chopped fresh thyme
- 3 tablespoons chopped fresh basil
- 1/4 cup kalamata olives
- 1/4 cup chopped fresh parsley
- Salt and black pepper to taste

## Directions

1. Heat oil in a skillet and add white wine.
2. Cook the chicken in it until brown for 4 minutes per side.
3. Then set the chicken aside.
4. Add the garlic to the same pan and cook for 20 seconds; add onions, and cook until tender.
5. Next, put in the tomatoes and bring them to a boil.
6. Add in ½ cup red wine.
7. Let it cook for 10 minutes.
8. Now put in basil and thyme, salt, and black pepper.
9. Cook over low heat.
10. Add olives and parsley and cook for 1 minute.
11. Then serve.

## CHAPTER NO 13

# 20 Soup Recipes

## 1. Lentil and Carrot Soup (DF) (GF)

| Preparation Time: 20 Minutes | Cooking Time: 6 Hours 10 Minutes | Servings: 2 |
|---|---|---|

### Ingredients

- 4 carrots, peeled and chopped
- 1 cup dried green lentils (rinsed)
- 1 small shallot (chopped finely)
- 2 teaspoons herbs, personal choice
- Salt and black pepper, to taste
- 6 cups chicken broth
- 2 cups rotisserie chicken, shredded
- ¼ cup coconut cream

### Directions

1. Combine the first 7 ingredients in a slow cooker.
2. Slow cook for 7 hours.
3. Add cream, covering it, and cook for 5 more minutes
4. Serve and enjoy.

## 2. Bean Soup (DF)

| Preparation Time: 20 minutes | Cooking Time: 6 hours | Servings: 4 |
|---|---|---|

### Ingredients

- 2 cups assorted beans, dried
- One can of whole plum tomatoes, un-drained
- 1 Yukon Gold potato, peeled
- 1 onion, peeled and chopped
- 1 cup carrot, cubed
- 2 garlic cloves, grated
- 2 teaspoons herbs, personal preference
- Salt and black pepper, to taste
- 6 cups of chicken broth
- 1 loaf of French bread

### Directions

1. Soak the beans in the water for a few hours.
2. Shift the beans to a slow cooker.
3. Then put in the tomatoes, potatoes, onion, carrots, garlic, seasoning, herbs, and stock.
4. Cook on low for 6 hours.

5. Once done, serve with French bread.

# 3. Lentils and Pumpkin Soup (GF)

 **Preparation Time:** 20 Minutes

 **Cooking Time:** 7 Hours

**Servings:** 4

## Ingredients

- 1.5-pound potatoes (diced into 1-inch pieces)
- 1 cup of Pumpkin
- 1 cup dried lentils (rinsed)
- 2 small onions, chopped
- 4 cloves garlic (minced)
- 1 teaspoon ginger (grounded)
- Salt and black pepper, to taste
- 2 cups of vegetable broth, low sodium
- 1 cup water

## Directions

1. Combine all the ingredients and let it cook for about 7 hours at low.
2. Once done, serve.

# 4. Slow Cook Cabbage Soup (GF)

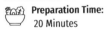 **Preparation Time:** 20 Minutes

 **Cooking Time:** 8 Hours 20 Minutes

 **Servings:** 4

## Ingredients

- 6 cups chicken stock
- 1 cup tomato paste
- 1 pound cabbage, shredded
- 2 carrots, chopped
- 1 onion, sliced
- 2 cups of great northern beans (rinsed, drained)
- 2 cloves garlic, minced
- 2 thyme sprigs, chopped
- 1 bay leaf
- Salt and black pepper, to taste
- Parmesan cheese (shredded, optional)

## Directions

1. Pour in the stock along with all the listed ingredients except cheese and thyme springs in a slow-cooked
2. Cook on low for 6 -7 hours.
3. Discard bay leaf and add thyme spring.
4. Add in the cheese after hours of cooking.
5. Cook for 5 more minutes.
6. Then serve.

# 5. White Bean Soup and Orange Slices (GF and DF)

 **Preparation Time:** 15 Minutes

 **Cooking Time:** 50 Minutes

 **Servings:** 4

## Ingredients

- 2 tablespoons of olive oil
- 4 carrots, sliced
- 5 celery sticks, sliced
- 1 onion, peeled and chopped
- ½ teaspoon dried oregano
- 1 bay leaf
- 3 orange segments
- 2 tablespoons tomato paste
- 14 ounces cannellini
- 2 cups water

## Directions

1. Heat olive oil in a large pot and cook onions for a few minutes.
2. Then add carrots and celery and let it cook for 5 more minutes.
3. Next, add the oregano, tomato paste, bay leaf, and orange segments.
4. Cook it for another 5 minutes.
5. Now add the beans, and pour in the 2 cups of water.
6. Cook it for 40 minutes, and then serve.

# 6. Cold Soup (DF)

 **Preparation Time:** 20 minutes

 **Cooking Time:** 10-12 minutes

 **Servings:** 4

## Ingredients

- 1.5 cups raw peanuts
- 2 cups coconut milk
- 1 cups broccoli, fresh or frozen

- ½ cup spinach, fresh or frozen
- ½ cup of leeks, sliced
- 4 garlic cloves, chopped
- ½ teaspoon ginger, grated
- 4 tablespoons of lemon juice
- Salt and black pepper, to taste

## Directions

1. Add veggies, salt, pepper, ginger, and garlic to a baking pan.
2. Let it cook for 10 minutes at 370 degrees F.
3. Once roasted, pulse it in a blender along with the remaining ingredients.
4. Serve cold.

# 7. Italian White Bean Soup (GF and DF)

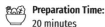 **Preparation Time:** 20 minutes     **Cooking Time:** 35 minutes     **Servings:** 4

## Ingredients

- 2 tablespoons olive oil
- 2 large peeled Potato (cut into ½-inch cubes)
- 2 carrots, sliced
- 1 onion, sliced
- 2 celery ribs (chopped)
- 1 medium zucchini (chopped)
- 1 teaspoon jalapeno pepper (chopped)
- 1 cans navy beans (rinsed, drained)
- 2 cups chicken broth
- 1 cup of tomato sauce
- 2 tablespoons thyme (minced)
- 2 tablespoons parsley (minced)

## Directions

1. Heat oil in a Dutch oven and add potatoes and carrots.
2. Cook for 10 minutes and add celery, zucchini, onion, and jalapenos.
3. Let it cook for 10 minutes.
4. Now add the remaining listed ingredients.
5. Cook it for 15 minutes.
6. Once the ingredients get soft and tender, serve them.

# 8. Chicken Cassoulet Soup (GF and DF)

 **Preparation Time:** 25 minutes  |  8 hours 5 minutes  |  2

**Cooking Time:**    **Servings:**

## Ingredients

- 1 pound turkey sausage
- 3 cups water
- 1 cup of kidney beans, rinsed, drained
- 1 cup of black beans, rinsed, drained
- 1 cup garbanzo beans, rinsed, drained
- 4 carrots, shredded
- 2 small onions, chopped
- 4 cup chicken broth
- 4 cloves garlic, minced
- 1 teaspoon thyme, minced
- ¼ teaspoon fennel seeds
- 1 teaspoon lavender flower, dried

## Directions

1. Cook the sausage in a skillet for 5 minutes.
2. Then add beans, garlic, carrots, water, onions, fennel, vermouth, chicken, and the remaining ingredients.
3. Cook it for 10 minutes and transfer it to a slow cooker.
4. Cover it with a lid and cook for 6 hours at low.
5. Once it's done, serve.

# 9. Summer Squash and White Beans Soup (GF)

 **Preparation Time:** 15 minutes  |   **Cooking Time:** 25 minutes  |   **Servings:** 2

## Ingredients

- 2 tablespoons butter, plant-based
- 2 tablespoons olive oil
- 2 sweet onions, chopped
- 2 cloves garlic, minced
- 4 yellow summer squash, cubed
- 6 cups of chicken broth
- 3 cups of cannellini beans, canned, rinsed, drained
- 1 cup parsley (minced)
- 1 tablespoon Tarragon
- ¾ cup Greek yogurt

## Directions

1. Heat olive oil in a skillet and cook onions,
2. Then add squash and let it cook for 10 minutes.

3. Pour in the broth and let it boil.
4. Let it cook with the lid on top for 10 minutes.
5. Now add the beans, parsley, tarragon, pepper, and salt.
6. Let it simmer, and use an immersion blender to blend it to a soupy consistency.
7. Top it with some Greek yogurt and serve.

## 10. Sausage and Cannellini Bean Soup (GF)

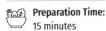 **Preparation Time:** 15 minutes |  **Cooking Time:** 25 Minutes |  **Servings:** 2

### Ingredients

- 4 Italian turkey sausages
- 2 small onions, chopped
- 4 cloves garlic
- 2 cans cannellini beans, rinsed, drained
- 1-1/2 cans chicken broth, reduced sodium
- 1 cup water
- ½ cup white wine
- ½ teaspoon pepper
- 1 bunch spinach, chopped
- 10 teaspoons Parmesan cheese (shredded)

### Directions

1. Cook the onion in a large saucepan in olive oil.
2. Then add sausages and let it cook for 3 minutes.
3. Now add garlic, drained beans, broth, water, beans, wine, and the seasoning.
4. Once the boil comes, add spinach.
5. Give it a garnish of cheese.

## 11. Cold Cucumber Soup (GF and DF)

 **Preparation Time:** 15 minutes |  **Cooking Time:** 0 Minutes |  **Servings:** 2

### Ingredients

For the soup

- 4 English cucumbers peeled, chopped
- 1.5 cups unsweetened almond milk
- 4 garlic cloves
- 6 fresh basil leaves
- 2 green onions
- 2 sweet apples, peeled and cored
- 1 lime, juice only
- Salt and black pepper, to taste

For the garnish:

- 1 cucumber
- 1 diced red pepper
- 4 slivered almonds

### Direction

- Add all the soup ingredients to a high-speed blender.
- Pulse it until smooth.
- Add some water if too thick.
- Let it chill in the refrigerator for a few hours.
- Then serve with toppings.

## 12. Lentil Tomato Soup (GF and DF)

 **Preparation Time:** 20 minutes |  **Cooking Time:** 40 minutes |  **Servings:** 4

### Ingredients

- 4 cups water
- 4 carrots, peeled and sliced
- 1 onion (chopped)
- 1-1/4 cups dried lentils (rinsed)
- 1 can of tomato paste
- 4 tablespoons parsley (minced)
- 2 tablespoons brown sugar
- 2 tablespoons white vinegar
- 1 teaspoon garlic salt
- ½ teaspoon thyme, dried

- ¼ teaspoon dill
- ½ tablespoon of tarragon
- Salt and black pepper, to taste

## Directions

1. Pour water, carrots, onions, and lentils into a large pot and simmer until a boil comes.
2. Reduce the heat and cook for 25 minutes with the lid on top.
3. Add in the remaining listed ingredients.
4. Return it to a boil, remove the lid, and simmer for 15 minutes.
5. Once done, serve.

# 13. Peas Pasta Soup (DF)

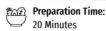 **Preparation Time:** 20 Minutes |  **Cooking Time:** 20-30 Minutes |  **Servings:** 2

## Ingredients

- 1/3 cup onion, chopped
- 2 tablespoons olive oil
- 2 cloves of garlic
- 1 tomato, chopped
- 4 cups chicken broth
- 1 cup water
- ½ teaspoon dried basil
- 1 teaspoon oregano
- ½ teaspoon celery flakes
- Salt and black pepper, to taste
- 2 cups of elbow macaroni, uncooked
- 1 cup of peas
- 1 tablespoon parsley (minced)

## Directions

1. Cook the onions in a skillet using olive oil.
2. Then add garlic and cook for 20 seconds.
3. Now add tomatoes and peas and simmer for 9 minutes.
4. Now add water, broth, and seasoning.
5. Let it cook for 5 minutes, then add the macaroni and boil until tender.
6. And serve it with a garnish of parsley.

# 14. Greek Soup with Orzo Pasta

 **Preparation Time:** 20 minutes |  **Cooking Time:** 15 minutes |  **Servings:** 4

## Ingredients

- 2 small white onions, peeled and sliced
- 2 tablespoons of olive oil
- 1 cup orzo pasta, uncooked
- 2 cans of whole tomatoes (coarsely chopped)
- 6 cups chicken broth
- 2 teaspoons dried oregano
- Salt and black pepper, to taste
- Feta cheese (crumbled, optional)
- Basil leaves as needed

## Directions

1. Sauté the onions in a skillet by heating olive oil in the skillet.
2. Now add tomatoes and let it cook for 5 minutes.
3. Then add orzo pasta and cook for 2 minutes
4. Pour in broth, and add listed seasonings.
5. Let it cook for 5 to 10 minutes.
6. Then add the feta cheese and basil leaves.
7. Serve.

# 15. Ravioli and Veggies Soup (DF)

 **Preparation Time:** 20 minutes |  **Cooking Time:** 20-25 minutes |  **Servings:** 4

## Ingredients

- 2 teaspoons of olive oil
- 2 cups bell pepper and onion mix, thawed and diced
- 4 cloves of garlic, minced
- 1/2 teaspoon crushed red pepper, or to taste (optional)
- 22 ounces can have crushed tomatoes, preferably fire-roasted
- 16 ounces of chicken broth
- 1 cup hot water
- 1 teaspoon marjoram
- 10 ounces of ravioli, whole-wheat
- 2 cups zucchini, peeled and cubed
- Salt and black pepper to taste

## Directions

1. Heat olive oil in a large Dutch oven and add pepper and onion mixture along with garlic and red peppers.
2. Cook it for 2 minutes.
3. Then add broth, water, and tomatoes.
4. Bring it to a rolling boil and add marjoram.
5. Now put in the ravioli and cook for 5 minutes, now add the zucchini and let it cook for 5 minutes.
6. Now season it with salt and black pepper, and enjoy.

# 16. Easy Salmon Soup (DF)

 **Preparation Time:** 20 minutes     **Cooking Time:** 35 minutes     **Servings:** 6

## Ingredients

- 4 tablespoons olive oil
- 4 green onions, chopped
- ½ green bell peppers
- 4 chopped garlic cloves
- ½ ounce dill
- 10 cups chicken broth
- 1 cup gold potatoes, peeled and chopped
- 1 carrot, peeled and chopped
- 1 teaspoon dry oregano
- 1 teaspoon coriander powder
- 1 teaspoon ground cumin powder
- Salt and black pepper, to taste
- 2 pounds of salmon fillets
- 1 loaf of French bread, sliced

## Directions

1. Heat some olive oil in a large pot and cook garlic until the aroma comes
2. Then add the green onions, garlic, and bell pepper and let it cook for 5 minutes.
3. Next, add dill, potatoes, carrots, and vegetable broth.
4. Let it simmer for 15 minutes, and add listed spices and seasoning.
5. Now add salmon and cook on low for 5 minutes.
6. In the end, add lemon zest and juice and let it stir
7. Serve the soup with French bread.

# 17. Roasted Cauliflower Soup (DF)

 **Preparation Time:** 20 minutes     **Cooking Time:**

---

35 minutes    **Servings:** 6

## Ingredients

- Ingredients for Soup:
- 1 large head of cauliflower
- 1.5 pounds of gold potatoes, scrubbed
- 4 medium yellow onions, papery skin removed
- 4 tablespoons fresh rosemary leaves
- 4 tablespoons olive oil
- Salt and ground black pepper to taste
- 4 tablespoons fresh lemon juice
- 6 cups vegetable stock
- Ingredients for toppings
- Croutons, as needed
- Toasted and chopped nuts, as needed.

## Directions

1. Cut the cauliflower into florets and add to an oil-greased baking sheet.
2. Add potatoes, and onions, aside the florets, and season it with salt, pepper, rosemary, and olive oil.
3. Rub the veggies well and add to the oven
4. Bake in the oven for 60 minutes at 350 degrees F.
5. Take out the cooked veggies and pour on top the lemon juice
6. Add all the listed ingredients to a blender and blend.
7. Add it to a large pot and pour it into stock
8. Simmer for 15 minutes, then serve with toppings

# 18. Coconut Pumpkin Soup (GF and DF)

 **Preparation Time:** 20 minutes     **Cooking Time:** 25-30 minutes    **Servings:** 4

## Ingredients

- 4 teaspoons of coconut oil
- 2 large onions, chopped
- 4 cloves of garlic, minced
- 1 teaspoon of ginger, grated
- Salt and black pepper to taste
- 2 teaspoons of thyme
- 1 teaspoon of Cayenne Pepper
- 4 cups Pumpkin, peeled and cubed
- 12 ounces of Coconut Cream, Unsweetened
- 2 cups Vegetable Stock

## Directions

1. Heat oil in a skillet and cook onions in it.
2. Then add the ginger and garlic and cook until the aroma comes.
3. Season it with cayenne pepper and thyme.
4. Now pour in the stock, coconut cream, and pumpkin.
5. Cook for 15 minutes.
6. Use an immersion blender to puree the soup.
7. Add the salt and pepper and serve.

# 19. Carrot and Orange Soup (GF and DF)

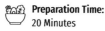 **Preparation Time:** 20 Minutes |  **Cooking Time:** 35 Minutes |  **Servings:** 2

## Ingredients

- 4 tablespoons of olive oil
- 4 white onions, finely chopped
- 1 pound of carrots, peeled, coarsely chopped
- 4 cups of vegetable liquid stock
- 2 cups of orange juice

## Directions

1. Heat olive oil in a large cooking pot.
2. Cook the onion in the olive oil for a few minutes.
3. Now add the carrots and cook for 3-5 minutes.
4. Now, pour in the vegetable stock.
5. Simmer it for 30 minutes until carrots get soft.
6. Let it cook for a while and blend into a puree of this soup,
7. Add orange juice. Stir and serve.

# 20. Sweet Potato Soup (GF and DF)

 **Preparation Time:** 20 Minutes |  **Cooking Time:** 35 Minutes |  **Servings:** 3

## Ingredients

- 4 teaspoons of olive oil
- 2 white onions, diced
- 1.5 pounds of orange sweet potato, peeled and chopped
- 4 medium carrots, peeled, roughly chopped
- 6 cups vegetable liquid stock
- Salt and black pepper to taste
- ½ cup fresn basil leaves

## Directions

1. Heat olive oil in a large pot and cook onions in it.
2. Once the onions get soft, add the sweet potato, carrot, and stock.
3. Add salt and black pepper.
4. Let it to a boil and cook for 25 minutes.
5. Once the carrots get soft, add the basil leaves.
6. Let it simmer for 5 minutes, and blend the soup with an immersion blender.
7. Once done, serve.

## CHAPTER NO 14

# 30 Beef, Lamb, Pork Recipes

## 1. Mediterranean Beef Pitas with Yogurt-Based Sauce (GF)

 **Preparation Time:** 25 Minutes |  **Cooking Time:** 20 Minutes |  **Servings:** 4

### Ingredients

1. 2 pounds of beef steak
2. 2 cups of Greek yogurt
3. 1 tablespoon lemon juice
4. 1 tablespoon crushed garlic
5. 1 cucumber
6. Salt and black pepper, to taste
7. 6 pita bread
8. 3/4 cup hummus
9. 10 cherry tomatoes
10. 1/2 cup Kalamata olives
11. 3 tablespoons feta cheese

### Directions

1. Mix a cup of yogurt, garlic, and lemon juice in a bowl.
2. Then place the beef in the yogurt and let it rest for at least 6 hours or overnight in the fridge.
3. While the beef is marinating, slice all the vegetables lengthwise. Slice the cucumbers and mix them in the yogurt mix.
4. Season with salt and pepper, and place the coated cucumbers in the fridge for a few hours.
5. Once the steak has rested in the fridge, take it out and cook it in the pan for around 12 minutes on high.
6. Coat the pita bread with hummus and layer it with cucumbers, tomatoes, and beef steaks.
7. Top it with more toppings of choice, like olives, feta cheese, and yogurt.
8. Once done, serve.

## 2. Mediterranean Pork Chops (GF and DF)

 **Preparation Time:** 35 Minutes |  **Cooking Time:** 25 Minutes |  **Servings:** 4

### Ingredients

- 4 pork loin chops, cut 1/2 inch cuts
- Salt and black pepper, to taste
- 1 teaspoon dried rosemary, crushed
- 4 cloves garlic, minced

## Directions

1. Start by preheating the oven to around 425 °F.
2. Place foil in a shallow roasting pan.
3. Season the chops with salt and pepper, and make sure to cover all the sides.
4. In a bowl, add rosemary and garlic and mix, rubbing it all over the chops once adequately mixed.
5. Arrange the pork chops in a shallow roasting pan and roast them for around 10 minutes.
6. Then reduce the temperature of the oven and bring it to 325 degrees F. keep roasting the chops for another 25 minutes or till the meat is no longer pink.

# 3. Mediterranean Beef Stew (GF and DF)

| Preparation Time: 20 Minutes | Cooking Time: 1 Hour 30 Minutes | Servings: 4 |
|---|---|---|

## Ingredients

- 2.5 pounds of stewing beef
- Salt and black pepper, to taste
- 4 tablespoons olive oil
- 1 large white onion
- 4 garlic cloves
- 2 cups tomatoes
- 2.5 cups beef stock
- 3 teaspoons fresh rosemary
- 1/2 teaspoon chili flakes
- 2 zucchinis
- 4 red capsicum/bell peppers
- 1/3 cup olives
- 4 tablespoons fresh parsley

## Directions

1. Start by dicing the meat into cubes and using a paper towel to dry them.
2. Season the meat chunks with salt and pepper and toss to coat evenly.
3. In a saucepan, heat oil over medium heat and add the beef chunks, cooking them till brown.

4. When done, take the beef chunks out and set them aside.
5. Add onions to the pan and sauté them for around 2 minutes.
6. Next, add the beef chunks to the pan and cook them with garlic and sautéed onions.
7. Then add in tomatoes, rosemary, and beef stock.
8. Mix everything and let it cook for around 1 hour.
9. Next, mix in zucchini and capsicum and cook them for 20 minutes.
10. In the end, mix olives and parsley in the pan and serve with a side of rice or noodles.

# 4. Pork with Greek Salad and Tzatziki (GF and DF)

| Preparation Time: 15 Minutes | Cooking Time: 18-22 Minutes | Servings: 2 |
|---|---|---|

## Ingredients

- Souvlaki:
- 1 pound pork chops
- ½ teaspoons ground cumin
- 1 teaspoon paprika powder
- Corn oil, as needed
- 2 teaspoons of balsamic Vinegar
- 1 cup Greek yogurt
- 2 sweet peppers, chopped
- Ingredients for Greek salad
- 1 cucumber, peeled and chopped
- 2 small onions
- 6 tomatoes, chopped
- ¼ cup feta cheese
- 1/8 cup Greek olives, chopped
- 20 green chili peppers, chopped
- Wine vinegar, splash
- Tzatziki sauce
- 1 cucumber
- 1 cup geek Yogurt
- 2 garlic cloves, minced

## Directions

1. Start by preheating the oven to around 400 degrees F.
2. Mix yogurt, oil, cumin, paprika, vinegar, salt, and pepper in a bowl.
3. Toss the pork into the bowls and set it aside to marinate.

4. Once marinated for enough time, take the meat and skewer it on a skewer.
5. Add all the ingredients for the Greek salad to a bowl and toss to mix evenly.
6. Slice the bell peppers and add them to the tzatziki mix.
7. Place the souvlaki and pepper in the oven and cook it for around 18 minutes.
8. When done, serve them with the side of Greek salad made earlier.

# 5. Lamb Chops with Pistachio Gremolata (GF and DF)

 **Preparation Time:** 15 Minutes   **Cooking Time:** 12 Minutes   **Servings:** 4

## Ingredients

- 1/3 teaspoon cumin powder
- ½ teaspoon coriander powder
- Salt and black pepper, to taste
- ⅛ Teaspoon cinnamon powder
- 6 lamb chops
- Cooking spray for greasing
- 2tablespoons chopped pistachios
- 4tablespoons chopped parsley
- 2 tablespoons chopped cilantro
- 2 teaspoons lemon zest
- 4 chopped garlic cloves or minced

## Directions

1. Start by heating oil in a skillet over medium heat.
2. Rub a mixture of cinnamon, coriander, salt, pepper, and cumin powder on the lamb chops and place them in the skillet.
3. Cook the lamb chops for around 8 to 12 minutes or till browned.
4. Once done, shift the chops to a serving plate and serve with a garnish of all remaining ingredients.

# 6. Garlic-Rosemary Lamb Pita (GF)

**Preparation Time:** 15 Minutes    10 Minutes    **Servings:** 2    **Cooking Time:**

## Ingredients

- 2 teaspoons olive oil
- 1 tablespoon rosemary
- 1 teaspoon crushed garlic
- Salt and black pepper, to taste
- 1.5 pounds lamb, without bones
- 1 ½ cups cucumber
- 1tablespoonlemon juice
- 2 cups Greek yogurt
- 4 pita bread
- 1 cup hot sauce, or as needed

## Directions

1. Start by heating oil over medium heat in a skillet.
2. Season the lamb chops with salt, pepper, garlic, and chopped rosemary.
3. Place the lamb chops over the skillet and cook for around 10 minutes.
4. Then mix yogurt, lemon juice, salt, pepper, and chopped cucumbers.
5. Serve the lamb chops with the yogurt and a side of pita bread.

# 7. Lamb lettuce Wraps (GF)

 **Preparation Time:** 12 Minutes   **Cooking Time:** 15-20 Minutes   **Servings:** 4

## Ingredients

- 2 teaspoons oil
- 2 cups of white onion
- 2 teaspoon chopped garlic
- 2 teaspoons cinnamon powder
- Salt and black pepper, to taste
- 2 pounds of lamb chops, boneless and cut thinly
- ½ cup parsley
- ½ cup tomato
- ½ cup cucumber
- 1 cup Greek yogurt
- 1 cup red pepper hummus
- 10 lettuce leaves
- 2 tablespoons mint leaves
- 2 tablespoons pine nuts

## Directions

1. Start by cutting the vegetables and cooking them in a skillet with oil over medium heat.

2. Cook the onions, garlic, cinnamon, salt, pepper, and lamb chops in the skillet for around 12 minutes.
3. Meanwhile, mix parsley, tomato, and cucumber in a bowl.
4. In another bowl, mix yogurt and hummus.
5. Arrange lettuce leaves over a serving plate and place the lamb chops over it. Top the chops with hummus, mint leaves, and pine nuts, and serve with the side of cucumber and tomato mixture.

# 8. Beef Kofta Patties

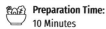 **Preparation Time:** 10 Minutes |  **Cooking Time:** 6-10 Minutes |  **Servings:** 4

## Ingredients

- Cooking spray
- 1.5 pound beef, grounded
- 1/3 cup parsley leaves
- 1/3 cup cilantro
- 2 tablespoons of grated ginger
- 2 teaspoons coriander powder
- ½ teaspoon cumin powder
- ¼ teaspoon of cinnamon powder
- 2 cups English cucumber
- ½ tablespoon rice vinegar
- 4 cups Greek yogurt
- 1 tablespoon lemon juice
- Salt and black pepper, to taste
- 2 pita bread

## Directions

1. Start by greasing the bottom of a pan with cooking spray.
2. Mix cilantro, parsley, ginger, ground beef, coriander, cinnamon, and cumin in a bowl.
3. From the batter, make a few patties and arrange them on the pan, cooking in a bowl.
4. Mix yogurt, lemon juice, salt, and pepper in another bowl.
5. Serve the beef patties with the cucumber salad, pita bread, and yogurt sauce.

# 9. Quick Lamb Kofta with Harissa Yogurt Sauce

 **Preparation Time:** 25 Minutes |  **Cooking Time:** 30 Minutes |  **Servings:** 2

## Ingredients

- 1 cup jasmine rice
- 1 teaspoon saffron
- 4 tablespoons onions
- 2 tablespoons cilantro
- 4 tablespoons onion
- 4 tablespoons Greek yogurt
- ½ b teaspoon cumin powder
- 1/3 teaspoon coriander powder
- 1 teaspoon turmeric powder
- 1-1/2 teaspoons chopped garlic
- Salt and black pepper
- 1.5-pound lamb, minced
- Cooking spray, as needed

### Sauce ingredients

- 1 cup roasted red bell pepper
- 1/4 teaspoon cumin powder
- ½ teaspoon chopped garlic
- ¼ teaspoon crushed red or green pepper
- 4 tablespoons of olive oil
- 2 tablespoons of lemon juice

## Directions

1. Start by cooking the rice in a pot of saffron water according to the instructions on the packaging.
2. When cooked, add chopped green onions over it and set aside.
3. Add cilantro, yogurt, cumin, coriander, salt, pepper, lamb, garlic, and turmeric powder to a bowl.
4. Once properly mixed, take the mixture and patties using it.
5. Place the patties in a skillet with oil over medium heat and cook them for around 10 minutes.
6. Make sure to flip them halfway in the cooking to ensure an even cook throughout.
7. Meanwhile, add all the ingredients for the sauce to a bowl and mix them.
8. Once the patties are cooked, take them out and serve with the sauce and rice.

# 10. Meat Loaf with Arugula Salad

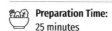 **Preparation Time:** 25 minutes |  **Cooking Time:** 50 minutes |  **Servings:** 4

## Ingredients

- 12 ounces of ground beef
- 12 ounces ground lamb
- 1 cup breadcrumbs
- 1 cup red onion
- 4 teaspoon mint leaves
- 4 teaspoon thyme
- Salt, to taste
- ¼ teaspoon mixed spice
- ¼ teaspoon crushed red pepper
- 6 crushed garlic cloves
- 2 small organic eggs, whisked
- Cooking spray, as needed
- 1.5 cup Greek yogurt
- 6 ounces feta cheese
- 1 tablespoon of mint and thyme
- 2 tablespoons lemon juice
- 2 tablespoons extra-virgin olive oil
- Black pepper, to taste
- 2cups arugula leaves
- 2 cups cucumber

## Directions

1. Start by preheating the oven to around 400 degrees F.
2. Add the first four ingredients to the bowl and mix them thoroughly.
3. Then mix mint, thyme, spices, salt, red pepper, garlic, and eggs in the bowl.
4. Grease the baking tray with oil, make loaves of the meat mixture and place them on a baking tray.
5. Cook it for 60 minutes.
6. While cooking, mix lemon juice, feta cheese, mint, thyme, and yogurt in a food blender and blend them till a smooth paste is formed.
7. Toss baby arugula and cucumber with oil, salt, and pepper.
8. Once everything is prepared, serve them on a serving plate.

# 11. Superfast Kofta

|  Preparation Time: 20 Minutes |  Cooking Time: 16-20 Minutes |  Servings: 4 |
| --- | --- | --- |

## Ingredients

- 1 cup onion
- 1 Cup breadcrumbs
- ½ cup mint
- 6 tablespoons tomato paste

- 2 teaspoons crushed garlic
- Salt, to taste
- 1 teaspoon cumin powder
- ½ teaspoon cinnamon powder
- ½ teaspoon red pepper
- ½ Teaspoon allspice powder
- 1.5-pound ground beef
- 2 eggs
- Cooking spray
- 12 slices of plum tomato
- 6 pita bread
- ½ cup Greek yogurt

## Directions

1. Start by preheating the oven for 3 minutes.
2. Add the first 12 ingredients to a bowl and mix it.
3. Once mixed, take the batter and make around 8 patties.
4. Coat the bottom of a pan with cooking spray and place the patties in it.
5. Place the pan in the oven and broil the patties for around 8 minutes, making sure to flip them halfway through the cooking process.
6. Serve the patties with pita bread topped with yogurt and tomato slices.

# 12. Lamb Chops with Farro, And Vinaigrette

|  Preparation Time: 15 Minutes |  Cooking Time: 15-20 Minutes |  Servings: 3 |
| --- | --- | --- |

## Ingredients

- Oil spray for greasing
- 6 lamb chops
- 2 cups precooked farro
- Salt and black pepper, to taste
- 2 teaspoons lemon zest
- 1 tablespoon lemon juice
- 4 tablespoons extra-virgin olive oil
- 2 tablespoons shallots
- 2 teaspoon honey
- 2 teaspoons Dijon mustard
- 2 cups of arugula

## Directions

1.  Start by coating a grill pan with cooking spray.
2.  Season the lamb chops with a generous amount of salt and pepper.
3.  Once seasoned, place the chops in the gill and cook them for 8 minutes, flipping them halfway to ensure an even cook.
4.  While the chops are cooking, make the faro according to the instructions on the back of the packaging.
5.  Add the following six ingredients to a bowl, season them with salt and black pepper, and mix everything.
6.  Then add sauce, faro, and arugula leaves to the bowl and mix them.
7.  Arrange the chops on a serving plate and serve with a serving of faro and dressing.

# 13. Orange-Balsamic Lamb Chops (GF and DF)

 **Preparation Time:** 15 Minutes
 **Cooking Time:** 12-15 Minutes
 **Servings:** 2

## Ingredients

- 4 teaspoons olive oil
- 2 tablespoons of lemon juice
- 2 teaspoons orange zest
- 1 tablespoon orange juice
- 6 lamb chops
- Salt and black pepper, to taste
- Oil spray for greasing
- 2 tablespoons balsamic vinegar

## Directions

1.  Start by mixing olive oil and lemon juice and coating the lamb chops.
2.  Then generously season them with salt and pepper.
3.  Coat the bottom of a pan with cooking spray and place the lamb chops on it, cooking it for 6 minutes over medium heat.
4.  While the chops are cooking, mix orange juice, vinegar, and orange zest in a saucepan and bring it to a boil.
5.  Once thickened, remove the sauce from the heat.
6.  Once the chops are cooked, place them on a serving plate and serve with a drizzle of vinegar syrup.

# 14. Lamb and Beet Meatballs

 **Preparation Time:** 25 Minutes
 **Cooking Time:** 10- 12 Minutes
 **Servings:** 4

## Ingredients

- 1cup cooked beets
- 1/2 cup bulgur
- 1 teaspoon cumin powder
- Kosher salt and black pepper, to taste
- 1 0 ounces ground lamb
- 3-ounce almond flour
- 3 tablespoons olive oil
- 1 cup grated cucumber
- 1 cup sour cream
- 2 tablespoons mint leaves
- 2 tablespoons lemon juice
- 4 cups mixed greens

## Directions

1.  Start by preheating the oven to around 400 ° F.
2.  Add the beets to a food processor and blend them with cumin, salt, pepper, lamb meat, flour, and bulgur.
3.  Take the mixture and form around six meatballs with it.
4.  Heat oil over medium heat in a skillet and add the meatballs to it, cooking them for 5 minutes per side.
5.  Mix mint leaves, lemon juice, sour cream, and cucumbers in another bowl.
6.  When done, place the meatballs on a serving plate and serve them with the sour cream mix and mixed greens.

# 15. Mediterranean Lamb Chops (GF and DF)

 **Preparation Time:** 25 Minutes
 **Cooking Time:** 15 Minutes
 **Servings:** 2

## Ingredients

- 4 tablespoons olive oil
- 6 lamb chops
- Salt and black pepper, to taste
- 6 plum tomatoes
- 2 garlic cloves
- 1 tablespoon of fennel
- 3 tablespoons lemon juice
- 1 tablespoon oregano
- 1 cup of arugula

## Directions

1. Start by preheating the oven to around 400 degrees F.
2. Add half of the oil to a skillet and heat it over medium heat.
3. Season the chops generously with salt and pepper and place them on the skillet, cooking them for 4 minutes or till browned.
4. Once browned, arrange the chops on a baking dish with parchment paper and place them in the oven for 8 minutes.
5. While the chops are cooking, add tomatoes, fennel, lemon juice, oregano, garlic, and the leftover oil to a bowl and mix them.
6. Once the chops are done, serve them with a side of arugula, fennel, and tomato mixture.

# 16. Mediterranean Pork with Olives (GF and DF)

 **Preparation Time:** 35 Minutes   **Cooking Time:** 30-35 Minutes   **Servings:** 2-4

## Ingredients

- 4 teaspoons of olive oil
- 8 bone-in pork chops, 3/4 inch thick
- 2 small onions, chopped
- 4 cloves garlic, finely chopped
- 1/2 cup dry beef broth
- 10 ounces of Pasta Sauce
- 1/3 cup ripe olives, pitted and sliced
- A few pinches of ground cinnamon

## Directions

1. Start by heating olive oil over medium heat in a 12-inch skillet.
2. Place the chops in it and sear them till brown.
3. Once the desired color is achieved, take them off the pan and set them aside.
4. Add onions and garlic to the same skillet and cook until the onions are tender.
5. Then pour wine into the pan and bring it to a boil, deglazing the pan.
6. Place the chops back in the skillet and add the remaining ingredients.
7. Bring it to a simmer and cover it with a lid, cooking for 20 minutes.

8. When done, serve the chops with cooked rice and a garnish of rosemary and olives.

# 17. Beef and Lamb Kofta Lettuce Wraps

 **Preparation Time:** 25 Minutes   **Cooking Time:** 25-35 Minutes   **Servings:** 2

## Ingredients

- 2 bread slices, crumbled
- 6 ounces ground beef
- 4 tablespoons red onion
- 4 tablespoons parsley
- 6 ounces ground lamb
- ½ tablespoon mint
- ½ teaspoon cinnamon powder
- 2 teaspoon allspice powder
- 2 small organic eggs
- Salt and black pepper, to taste
- ½ tablespoon of vegetable oil
- 1.5 cups Greek yogurt
- 4 tablespoons cucumber
- 4 tablespoons of onions, chopped
- 1 cup brown rice
- ½ teaspoon paprika powder
- 4 tablespoons of olive oil for cooking

## Directions

1. Start by crumbling the bread in a food blender.
2. Add the crumbs to the bowl and mix it with parsley, beef, onions, lamb, and the following five ingredients.
3. Take the mixture and make around 8 patties with it.
4. Arrange the patties in the skillet and cook them for 6 minutes per side in olive oil.
5. Meanwhile, add yogurt, salt, pepper, cucumber, and onions to a bowl and mix.
6. Then cook the brown rice according to the instructions on the package.
7. Once everything is done, serve the patties with a side of yogurt and rice.

# 18. Mediterranean Beef Stir-Fry (GF and DF)

 **Preparation Time:** 12 Minutes   **Cooking Time:** 15 Minutes   **Servings:** 4

## Ingredients

- 4 red sweet peppers
- 4 zucchinis, peeled and chopped
- 8 button mushrooms sliced
- 3 small onions, peeled and chopped
- 2 crushed garlic cloves
- 2 tomatoes, chopped
- 1 cup beef, sliced
- 4 tablespoons olive oil, divided
- Salt and black pepper, to taste

## Directions

1. Start by slicing the vegetables, except for the zucchini, into long and thin slices.
2. For the zucchini, slice them in rounds. Slice the mushrooms in rounds and set them aside.
3. Dice the beef and cook it in the frying pan with foil for around 5 minutes.
4. Set the beef aside and add onions to the pan, sautéing them with oil for around 2 minutes.
5. Next, add the mushrooms, zucchini, and peppers to the pan, cooking them for another 10 minutes.
6. Mix everything and add garlic and tomatoes in.
7. Season the vegetables with salt and pepper.
8. When cooked, add the beef to the pan and toss with the vegetables and serve.

# 19. Beef with Artichokes (GF and DF)

| 9. Preparation Time: 20 minutes | Cooking Time: 5 hours 5 minutes | Servings: 4 |
|---|---|---|

## Ingredient

- 2 tablespoons grape seed oil
- 2 pounds of beef stew
- 2 cans of artichoke hearts
- 2 small onions, chopped
- 4 garlic cloves
- 6 cups of beef broth
- 2 cans of tomato sauce
- 1 can of diced tomatoes
- 1 cup Kalamata olives
- 2 teaspoons dried oregano
- 1 teaspoon parsley

- 1 teaspoon basil
- 1 teaspoon cumin powder

## Directions

1. Start by heating oil in a large skillet or a cooking pan.
2. Place the beef in a pan and sear it on both sides for 2 minutes.
3. Once browned, add the beef to a slow cooker and cook it with all the other ingredients listed.
4. Let the beef slowly cook for at least 5 hours.
5. When done, take it out and enjoy.

# 20. Beef with Kale Salad (DF)

| Preparation Time: 20 Minutes | Cooking Time: 35 Minutes | Servings: 4 |
|---|---|---|

## Ingredients

- 4 beef steaks
- Salt and black pepper, to taste
- 6 crushed garlic cloves
- 1 cup beef broth
- 2 cups Farro
- 2 cups kale
- 1 cup dried cranberries
- 6 tablespoons almonds
- 6 teaspoons lemon juice

## Directions

1. Start by mixing garlic, salt, and pepper and coating the beef.
2. Add farro, beef broth, garlic, and pepper to a saucepan.
3. Place the beef in and cook it for around 15 minutes.
4. Then add cranberries, kale, sliced almonds, and lemon juice.
5. Season it with salt, and broil it for around 16 minutes.
6. When done, take it out and serve.

# 21. Mediterranean Beef with Olives and Feta (GF)

| Preparation Time: 20 Minutes | Cooking Time: 3 Hours | Servings: 4 |
|---|---|---|

## Ingredients

- 2 pounds beef, cubed
- 2 cans of tomatoes seasoned with chili
- 1 cup assorted olives
- Salt and black pepper, to taste
- 2 cups cooked basmati rice
- 2 cups crumbled feta cheese

## Directions

1. Start by slow cooking the beef with tomatoes and olives for about 6 hours with a lid on inside a slow cooker.
2. After that, season it with some salt and serve with a side of rice and an optional cheese topping.

# 22. Mediterranean Ground Beef Stir Fry(GF)

 **Preparation Time:** 20 Minutes  **Cooking Time:** 15-25 Minutes  **Servings:** 2

## Ingredients

- 2 tablespoons olive oil
- 2 red bell peppers
- 2 cups cherry tomatoes
- 6 ounces of baby spinach
- 6 garlic cloves
- 2 green onions
- 1.5-pound ground beef
- 2 teaspoons dried oregano
- Salt and black pepper, to taste
- 6 tablespoons feta

## Directions

1. Start by heating oil in a pan over medium heat and adding bell peppers and cherry tomatoes once the oil is hot.
2. Next, mix in the garlic and cook it for around 1 minute.
3. Then mix in spinach and onions and cook them for around 3 minutes.
4. Once the spinach is wilted, remove the pan from heat and shift the vegetables to a plate.
5. Place the beef on the pan and brown it on all sides, then add the vegetables back in and toss to mix.
6. Once mixed, serve the beef with a garnish of feta cheese.

# 23. Beef with Spinach in the

# Skillet (GF and DF)

 **Preparation Time:** 20 minutes  **Cooking Time:** 40 Minutes  **Servings:** 4

## Ingredients

- 1.5 pounds beef
- 1 cup white onions, chopped
- ½ cup olive oil
- 1 teaspoon dry mint
- 1/2 cup dill
- 1.5 cup chopped tomatoes
- Salt and pepper, to taste
- 2 pounds spinach
- 1/2 cup of water

## Directions

1. Start by heating olive oil over medium heat in a pot.
2. Add the beef to the pot once the oil is hot and cook it with the onions, mint, dill, tomatoes, salt, and pepper for around 20 minutes.
3. Mix in spinach and cook it for another 20 minutes.
4. When done, shift the beef and vegetables to a serving plate and serve.

# 24. Beef Roast with Feta (GF)

 **Preparation Time:** 30 minutes  **Cooking Time:** 1 hour 30 minutes  **Servings:** 2

## Ingredients

- 2tablespoons butter, plant-based
- 2.5cups boneless beef
- 1 onion
- 4 garlic cloves
- 1/2 cup beef stock
- 1/2 cup orange juice
- 1 teaspoon cinnamon
- Salt and black pepper, to taste
- Mediterranean topping
- 6 tablespoons mint leaves
- 1/2 cup parsley
- 1/2 cup raisins
- 1/2 cup toasted almonds
- 1tablespoonorange zest
- 1/2 cup Italian tomatoes
- 1/2 cup Feta

- Salt and black pepper, to taste

## Directions

1. Start by preheating the oven to around 340 degrees F.
2. In a pan, melt some butter and roast veal in it.
3. Then add beef stock, garlic, onions, cinnamon, and orange juice.
4. Season everything with a good amount of salt and pepper and cook it for around 1 hour.
5. While cooking, add all the listed toppings to a bowl and toss them together to mix.
6. When done, shift everything to a serving plate and serve.

## 25. Mediterranean Beef Pockets (DF)

 **Preparation Time:** 10 Minutes  **Cooking Time:** 10 Minutes  **Servings:** 4

## Ingredients

- 1 pound beef steak
- 2 tablespoons of olive butter
- 14 cup olive oil
- 2 cucumbers
- 4 red onions
- ½ cup parsley leaves
- 1 cup kalamata olives
- 4 tablespoons lemon juice
- Salt & black pepper
- 2 pocket bread
- 1 cup tomato chutney

## Directions

7. Use a meat mallet and pound the beef steak inside a plastic bag.
8. Heat olive oil and butter in a frying pan and add the steak once hot.
9. Cook the steak for around 4 minutes on each side.
10. While cooking, add onions, oil, lemon juice, olives, cucumber, parsley, salt, and pepper to a bowl and mix them thoroughly.
11. Place the beef steak inside a pita bread pocket and add a dollop of cucumber mixture and tomato sauce over it.
12. Cover it using a foil and serve.

## 26. Mediterranean Pork and Orzo(DF)

 **Preparation Time:** 20 Minutes  **Cooking Time:** 25-30 Minutes  **Servings:** 2

## Ingredients

- 1 pound pork tenderloin
- 1 teaspoon coarsely ground pepper
- 2 tablespoons olive oil
- 2 quarts water
- 1 cups uncooked orzo pasta
- Salt, to taste
- 1 cup fresh baby spinach
- 1.5 cups grape tomatoes, halved
- 1/2 cup crumbled feta cheese

## Directions

1. Start by coating the pork with pepper and dicing it into 1-inch cubes.
2. Heat oil over medium heat in a nonstick skillet and cook the pork cubes for around 8 to 10 minutes.
3. While the pork is cooking, boil water in a Dutch pot and add orzo and salt to it once it begins to boil.
4. Cook the orzo for around 8 minutes without a lid.
5. Then mix in spinach and cook for another minute or till wilted.
6. Then add tomatoes to the pan with the pork and add the orzo.
7. Sprinkle cheese over them and serve.

## 27. Beef with Lemon, Capers & Leeks (GF and DF)

 **Preparation Time:** 15 minutes  **Cooking Time:** 25 minutes  **Servings:** 3

## Ingredient

- 6 beef cutlets
- Salt and black pepper, to taste
- 1/2 cup flour
- 4teaspoon extra-virgin olive oil
- 5 leeks
- 1 cup chicken broth
- 4 garlic cloves
- 4 tablespoons capers
- 2 teaspoons lemon zest

- 4 tablespoons lemon juice
- 4 tablespoons parsley

## Directions

1. Start by seasoning the cutlets with a good amount of salt and pepper.
2. Add flour to a bowl and toss the seasoned beef until evenly coated.
3. Heat olive oil in a skillet over medium heat and cook the beef in it for around 6 minutes.
4. When done, shift them to a plate and heat 2 tablespoons of oil in the pan.
5. Add the leeks to the pan and cook it for around 8 minutes.
6. Then pour in the broth, mix in the garlic and bring it to a boil, letting it boil for around 2 minutes.
7. Mix in lemon zest, lemon juice, salt, pepper, and parsley.
8. Then add the beef to the pan, toss and cook.
9. Once done, shift the beef to a serving plate and serve with the side of leeks, capers, and a drizzle of dressing.

## 28. Mediterranean Pork Kabobs(GF and DF)

 **Preparation Time:** 20 Minutes  **Cooking Time:** 35 Minutes  **Servings:** 4

### Ingredients

- 4 boneless pork chops
- 8 ounces of marinated artichoke hearts
- ½ red bell pepper, sliced
- 1 tablespoon hot pepper sauce
- 1 tablespoon oregano
- 2 tablespoons lemon juice
- Salt and black pepper, to taste

### Directions

1. Start by dicing the pork into 1-inch cubes and adding them to a zip lock bag.
2. Next, drain the artichokes and save the marinade for later use.
3. Pour the marinade into the zip lock bag with the other ingredients and close it.
4. Let it rest for around 30 minutes.

5. Once everything has marinated for enough time, take it out and place it over a grill with coals heated to medium heat.
6. Arrange the artichokes, pork, and peppers on the grill and cook them for around 15 minutes.
7. Once done, shift it to a serving bowl and serve.

## 29. Mediterranean Pork Stew(GF)

 **Preparation Time:** 20 Minutes  **Cooking Time:** 8 hours  **Servings:** 4

### Ingredients

- 1.5 pounds pork loin roast boneless, cut into 1-inch pieces)
- ½ cup almond flour
- 1 teaspoon ground cinnamon
- 1 teaspoon dried thyme
- 1.5 cups pearl onions (frozen)
- 16 ounces of chicken broth
- ½ cup dry red wine
- 2 teaspoons of honey
- 2 teaspoons of balsamic vinegar

### Directions

1. Mix flour with thyme and cinnamon in a bowl.
2. Add the pork to the flour and toss to coat it evenly.
3. Mix broth, wine, honey, and vinegar in a bowl.
4. Add the pork to a slow cooker, add onions and broth, mix with the meat, and cook everything on low for around 8 hours.
5. When done, serve the stew with the side of pasta or rice and a garnish of goat cheese.

## 30. Grilled Pork Roast (GF and DF)

 **Preparation Time:** 30 Minutes  **Cooking Time:** 22-25 Minutes  **Servings:** 4

### Ingredients

6. 2 pounds pork loin roast, boneless
7. 2 lemons
8. 2 cloves garlic (peeled)
9. 1/2 cup rosemary leaves (fresh)
10. 1/2 cup sage leaves (fresh)

11. Salt and black pepper, to taste

## Directions

12. Start by roasting the pork dry.
13. Add all the remaining ingredients to a food blender and blend them till finely blended.
14. Coat the roast with the blended seasoning and place it over indirect heat at medium heat.
15. Close the grill and let the roast cook for around 22 minutes.
16. Once the internal temperature reaches 145, let it rest for around 10 minutes before serving.

# 28-DAY MEAL PLAN

| Days | Breakfast | Lunch | Dinner |
|------|-----------|-------|--------|
| 1 | Strawberry-Thyme Millet Bowl (GF and DF) | Greek Spinach Pies | Baked Chicken Breast (GF and DF) |
| 2 | Migas (GF) | Mediterranean Pie (GF) | Turkey Mediterranean Casserole on a Plate |
| 3 | Sandwiches Filled With Egg, Cheese, Spinach, and Tomato | Classic Mediterranean Pie | Mediterranean Turkey Sandwich (GF) |
| 4 | Vegetable Scrambled Eggs (GF) | Chicken Pie | One-Pot Chicken Pesto Pasta with Asparagus |
| 5 | Brioche Bread (GF) | Mediterranean Meat Pies | Mediterranean Chicken & Chickpea Soup (GF and DF) |
| 6 | Cheesy Mushrooms and Egg Tartine | Cauliflower Tapas | Sicilian Olive Chicken (GF and DF) |
| 7 | Blueberries Bowl | Lemony Mediterranean Rice (GF) | Shakshuka Recipe |
| 8 | Sunny-Side-Up Eggs on Garlicky Greens (GF) | Chickpeas and Rice with Tahini (DF) | Mediterranean Chicken with Brussels sprouts |
| 9 | Nectarine Bruschetta (GF) | One Pot Pasta | Chicken with Orzo Salad (GF) |
| 10 | Spinach Crepes with Apples and Chickpeas (GF) | Chicken Parmesan Pasta | Baked Mustard and Balsamic Chicken (GF and DF) |
| 11 | Mediterranean Homemade Croissant | Bruschetta Pasta | Quick Lamb Kofta with Harissa Yogurt Sauce |

| Days | Breakfast | Lunch | Dinner |
|------|-----------|-------|--------|
| 12 | Breakfast Pogaca | One-Pot Greek Pasta | Meat Loaf with Arugula Salad |
| 13 | Goat Cheese Egg Muffins with Spinach (GF) | Greek Spaghetti | Superfast Kofta |
| 14 | Breakfast Creamy Avocado Omelets (GF) | Creamy Pasta with Broccoli and Mushrooms | Lamb Chops with Farro, And Vinaigrette |
| 15 | Tomato and Egg Stacks (GF and DF) | Chicken Pesto Pasta with Broccoli | Orange-Balsamic Lamb Chops (GF and DF) |
| 16 | Avocado Smoothie (GF and DF) | Chicken and Kale Pasta with Lemon and Parmesan | Lamb and Beet Meatballs |
| 17 | Butternut Squash and Spinach Toast | Ravioli with Arugula & Pecorino | Mediterranean Lamb Chops (GF and DF) |
| 18 | Shakshuka (GF) | Simple Mediterranean Olive Oil Pasta | Tuna with Dijon Vinaigrette (GF and DF) |
| 19 | Sweet Potato and Spinach Frittata (GF) | Orange and Cranberry Rice | Mediterranean Seafood Stew (GF and DF) |
| 20 | Easy Savory Oatmeal Bowls | Greek Rice Pilaf | Mediterranean Pan-Roasted Salmon (GF and DF) |
| 21 | Blueberry-And-Mixed Nut Parfait (GF) | Simple Coconut Rice (DF) | Tuna, Egg, and Cheese (GF) |
| 22 | Strawberry-Thyme Millet Bowl (GF and DF) | Autumn Chestnut Rice (DF) | Mediterranean Style Shrimp Recipe (GF and DF) |
| 23 | Migas (GF) | Rice with Butternut Casserole | Mediterranean Grouper (GF) |
| 24 | Sandwiches Filled With Egg, Cheese, Spinach, and Tomato | Lemony Rice with Feta Cheese | Grilled Swordfish Recipe with a Mediterranean Twist (GF and DF) |
| 25 | Vegetable Scrambled Eggs (GF) | Mediterranean Cauliflower Fried Rice | Baked White Fish (GF and DF) |
| 26 | Brioche Bread (GF) | Rice, Potato, and Fish Mix (GF and DF) | Easy Shrimp Scampi (GF and DF) |
| 27 | Cheesy Mushrooms and Egg Tartine | Rice with Cashews and Pecans | Chicken Cassoulet Soup (GF and DF) |
| 28 | Blueberries Bowl | Grilled Chicken Tzatziki Sauce with Yellow Rice | Summer Squash and White Beans Soup (GF) |

# BONUS!

# Thanks! Find your gift here!

An extensive collection of Mediterranean air fryer meals to have even more Ideas, or make a gift. Send the Pdf to friends and family with a single Click on Whatsapp or Social Network. Enjoy!

# Note

Printed in Great Britain
by Amazon

16717722R00059